REGIONAL LONG WAVES, UNEVEN GROWTH, and THE COOPERATIVE ALTERNATIVE

REGIONAL LONG WAVES, UNEVEN GROWTH, and THE COOPERATIVE ALTERNATIVE

Douglas E. Booth

New York
Westport, Connecticut
London

Library of Congress Cataloging-in-Publication Data

Booth, Douglas E.
    Regional long waves, uneven growth, and the
cooperative alternative.

    Bibliography: p.
    1. Long waves(Economics) 2. Regional economic
disparities. 3. United States—Economic conditions—
Regional disparities. 4. Economic development.
I. Title.
HB3729.B66 1987   338.973   87-2348
ISBN 0-275-92567-6 (alk. paper)

Library of Congress Catalog Card Number: 87-2348
ISBN: 0-275-92567-6

First published in 1987

Praeger Publishers, 521 Fifth Avenue, New York, NY 10175
A division of Greenwood Press, Inc.

Printed in the United States of America

The paper used in this book complies with the Permanent
Paper Standard issued by the National Information Standards
Organization (Z39.48-1984).

10 9 8 7 6 5 4 3 2 1

CONTENTS

1

INTRODUCTION

In the 1950s and 1960s the New England and Middle Atlantic states suffered from employment growth rates well below the national level. At the same time, employment growth rates in the Midwest were only slightly below the national figures. In more recent years, however, this relative growth configuration has reversed itself, with the Midwest now suffering employment growth substantially below the national rate and the Northeast enjoying employment growth very close to the national rate. What explains this fundamental shift in employment growth patterns? Why is the northeastern regional economy experiencing a revival of growth while the midwestern economy is languishing?

The central thesis of this book is that regional economies, like national economies and the world economy, go through long waves of economic activity. Specifically, a region will experience a relatively lengthy period of economic growth close to or above the national rate followed by a relatively lengthy period of economic growth below the national rate. The northeastern regional economy has suffered from relatively slow economic growth since approximately the 1920s, and in the late 1970s and early 1980s appears to have shifted to the rapid-growth phase of a regional long wave. On the other hand, the midwestern economy has faced growth rates substantially below the national rate since the mid-1970s and thus appears to be entering the slow-growth phase of a regional long wave.[1] In comparison with the northeastern and midwestern states, the economies of other regions of the country are relatively young and either have not yet developed sophisticated urban manufacturing and service economies or are still in their first rapid-growth phase of a regional long wave.

What is the theoretical foundation of the regional long wave? Why does it exist? In order to understand the basis for a regional long wave, a brief review of the theory of long waves at the national and international levels is a useful starting point.

LONG WAVES IN ECONOMIC ACTIVITY

Long waves can be viewed as either price cycles or economic activity cycles.[2] Economists such as Kondratieff and Rostow suggest that the long-wave phenomenon is a price cycle, while others, such as Schumpeter, argue that it is an output cycle (Kondratieff 1935; Rostow and Kennedy 1979; Schumpeter 1939, 1961). Since the present work follows the latter tradition, the review of long-wave theory will be confined to consideration of the long wave in economic activity. There are really two issues to deal with in long wave analysis: Do long waves exist? If they do, what are their causes? Although the existence of long waves is still hotly debated, a recent study provides convincing evidence that they do (Van Duijn 1983, 147–64).

The long wave in economic activity can be divided into four phases: recovery, prosperity, recession, and depression. It is a cyclical fluctuation in the growth rate of output lasting anywhere from 40 to 60 years. The cycle is defined in terms of the growth rate of output rather than the absolute level of output. In the recovery phase the rate of economic growth begins to accelerate from its depression low. It reaches its maximum in the prosperity phase, begins to diminish in the recession phase, and reaches its lowest level in the depression phase (Van Duijn 1983, 135).

Like the issue of its existence, the underlying cause of the long wave is subject to heated debate. Some argue that long waves can be traced to cycles in infrastructure investment, while others suggest that long waves are caused by the clustering of innovations and industry life cycles. Those who accept the former view argue that an infrastructure investment cycle is generated by relatively long-lived capital investments found most frequently in the transportation sector.[3] Examples include rail lines, harbor facilities, waterways, highways, and civil transport aircraft. Infrastructure investment also includes investment in basic industrial facilities, such as refinery complexes, steel mills, and communications and power-generating facilities. During the depression phase of a long wave, very little infrastructure investment is undertaken because of excess capacity. Eventually, excess capacity in infrastructure is worked off, and new infrastructure investment is needed. After a time lag that results because the need for investment is not immediately recognized and time is required to allocate funds to investment projects, infrastructure investment accelerates and stimulates growth in aggregate demand and output. Growth of infrastructure investment spending carries the economy through recovery into prosperity. Such investment spending generally overshoots the long-term need, and excess capacity is the result. Once the presence of excess capacity is recognized, investment expenditures are reduced, leading initially to the recession phase and ultimately to the depression phase of the long wave.[4]

The alternative view suggests that long waves in economic activity can be explained by waves of innovations and industrial life cycles, and that cycles in infrastructure investment are the consequence of innovation waves. Schumpeter was the first to argue that long waves in economic activity could be explained by the bunching of basic innovations, where basic innovations are defined as those leading to the creation of new industries and new sectors (Schumpeter 1961; Van Duijn 1983, 97–106). Economic growth in the recovery and prosperity phases of the long wave, in Schumpeter's view, is led by new industries and sectors created by basic innovations. Basic innovations can include the introduction of a new good, the introduction of a new method of production, the opening of a new market, the development of a new source of supply for raw materials or semifinished goods, or the creation of a new organizational scheme in industry. The carrying out of the basic innovations is undertaken by the entrepreneur, who creates the needed organization structure for the new activity. In short, entrepreneurs carry out basic innovations that lead to the creation of new industries, and new industries serve as engines of economic growth.

Why would basic innovations necessarily occur in bunches, generating waves of rapid economic growth, and what would cause the recession and depression phases of the long wave? To summarize Schumpeter's argument very briefly, the kind of entrepreneurial talent necessary to carry out basic innovations is in very limited supply, and the success of a pioneering entrepreneur will open the way for others who are less talented by removing key barriers to further innovation. Consequently, innovation and the creation of new industries will appear in bunches. The success of a pioneer entrepreneur in a given industry or sector will stimulate the activity of others. Because pioneers are limited in supply, innovation will be uneven over time. Innovation and the development of new industries will result in a boom in capital investment that will lead the economy through the recovery and prosperity phases of the long wave. Prosperity, however, is self-destructive and does not last. The increased demand for investment goods in the newly created industries drives up the prices of capital goods for the older industries as well as the new, placing a squeeze on the profits of the old. In addition, the new industries begin to compete with the old for consumers' disposable income, causing profits and outputs in the latter industries to decline; and the increased entrance of new entrepreneurs begins to reduce the profits in the new industries. Also, entrepreneurs begin to pay back the debts they accumulated during the recovery and early prosperity phases, thereby reducing the amount of capital expenditures. The result is a movement from the prosperity to the recession and depression phases of the long wave.

Schumpeter's theory of the long wave has two key gaps in it. First, it does not really explain why innovation occurs in clusters and why a recovery from the depression will necessarily occur; second, it does not provide a completely convincing explanation for the movement from the prosperity to the recession and depression phases of the long wave (Van Duijn 1983, 103–06). Schumpeter does not make clear why, at the peak of the long wave, declining profits would necessarily lead to a decline in the growth rate of economic activity. Also, there is nothing in his theory that would necessarily preclude the uniform occurrence of innovation over time rather than in distinct bunches. Pioneer entrepreneurs could as easily enter the market and experience success at a uniform rate rather than in bunches at the beginning of a long wave. Finally, there appears to be no reason why recovery would necessarily occur from a depression, since the conditions would be poor for the starting of new business ventures by pioneer entrepreneurs.

Schumpeter's theory can be modified, however, to overcome these criticisms (Van Duijn 1983, 106–11; Mensch 1979). Basic innovations create new industries, and new industries go through life cycles involving an initial stage of rapid growth in output, a second stage of growth retardation, and in some cases a final stage of absolute decline in output (Burns 1934, 48–169; Van Duijn 1983, 220–32).

The retardation of growth occurs because markets for the new industries eventually become saturated. Given that basic innovations occur
in bunches and new industries are the engines of growth for long-
wave expansions, market saturation would explain the upper turning
point of a long wave. Retardation of growth in new industries would
reduce the overall rate of economic growth. A reduced rate of growth
in turn would reduce the level of capital investment, thereby causing
a further decline in economic growth. Why would a new set of basic
innovations and growth industries eventually develop in the depression phase of the long wave and bring about a recovery? In Mensch's
view, the depression phase forces investors to turn away from the
former growth industries now facing economic stagnation, and to
look for investment opportunities in new industries. The potential of
the previous batch of basic industries and growth industries will be
exhausted at this point, and desperate investors will now search out a
new set of basic innovations and growth industries (Van Duijn 1983,
109). With the development of a new set of growth industries, recovery in economic growth will take place.

While these modifications to Schumpeter's theory make it more
plausible, doubts can still be raised about its explanatory power (Van
Duijn 1983, 109–11, 129–43). Market saturation may not be enough
to bring on the depression phase of a long wave, and it is unlikely
that basic innovations and the creation of new industries will occur in
the depths of a depression. A synthesis of the infrastructure investment cycle, and the clustering of basic innovations and the creation
of new industries provides a more convincing explanation of the long
wave than each theory standing by itself. In the depths of the depression phase, infrastructure investment is allowed to depreciate because
of excess capacity and poor economic conditions. Eventually, re-
placement investment must be undertaken, and economic recovery
commences as a result. With improved economic conditions, basic
innovations can be undertaken. The resulting new set of high-growth
industries, along with infrastructure investment stimulated by the
creation of new industries, leads the economy into the prosperity
phase of the long wave. The amount of infrastructure investment undertaken overshoots the underlying need because investment decisions are made on the grounds that the high growth rates of the prosperity phase will be maintained, growth rates that cannot be sustained
in the long term because of market saturation. Once excess capacity
emerges, infrastructure investment spending collapses and the econo-

my moves into the depression phase. The depression phase generally lasts for a relatively long time because excess infrastructure capacity must be used up, and the former high-growth industries are facing market saturation and are no longer capable of being the engine that pulls the rest of the economy along.[5]

THE REGIONAL LONG WAVE

The long wave in economic activity at the national and international levels is thus dependent in part on waves of innovation that result in the creation of new high-growth industries. These industries in turn go through a life cycle of development characterized by initial rapid growth and eventual retardation of growth as their markets become saturated. A fundamental hypothesis of this book is that the regional long wave can also be explained by industrial life cycles and the creation of new high-growth industries. The central argument is that new industries emerge in regions of the country not already dominated by major industries that have risen to prominence in the recent past or in regions of the country that have suffered poor economic growth for an extensive period of time because of the economic decline of older industries. A given regional long wave is fundamentally determined by the life cycle of the industries that emerge at the beginning of the long wave. A set of high-growth industries is developed in a given region, the region experiences relatively rapid growth during the initial high-growth phase of the life cycles of these industries, and it experiences retardation of growth as these industries face the problem of market saturation. Even though such industries may not experience an absolute decline in output as markets become saturated, they are likely to reduce employment. As an industry matures and its technology stabilizes, competition will intensify as producers emerge in other regions or countries with lower wages. To remain competitive, the industry will invest in labor-saving technology or move its production facilities to locations with lower wages. In either case the result will be reduced employment.

In order for this theory of the regional long wave to be logically complete, an explanation of why new industries do not emerge in regions with established industries is needed. If in fact a new set of growth industries emerged alongside the old set of growth industries before declining employment was experienced in the latter, a decline in regional employment growth would not necessarily occur as the older industries experienced market saturation. The new set of growth industries would simply take up the mantle of growth from the old. The explanation for the absence of new industries at the end of a regional long-wave growth phase (briefly summarized here) is simple and will be outlined more fully in Chapter 2.

In regions with established industries, individuals who would otherwise start new businesses will be attracted to the easy life of managerial or professional positions offered by those industries. Consequently the rate of new business formation will be relatively low, thereby reducing the likelihood that a pioneering entrepreneur with a major basic innovation will emerge to provide the foundation stone for the creation of a new high-growth industry. However, once employment decline occurs in established industries, new business formation will accelerate as managerial and professional employment opportunities diminish in the region. Those with entrepreneurial abilities who desire to remain in the region will have little choice but to start new business ventures in order to earn a decent living. The resulting acceleration in new business formation will set the stage for the creation of new industries and a regional economic recovery. The period of new industry incubation can be lengthy, however, and a region will suffer poor economic growth and above-average unemployment for a substantial period of time before recovery takes place.

An obvious question to raise at this point in the discussion is the following: Why don't mature corporations faced with the prospect of saturated markets themselves develop new products that can serve as a basis for the development of new industries in regions experiencing a retardation of economic growth? The reasons why established enterprises in mature industries seldom create new growth industries are set out in detail in chapters 2 and 4. Simply stated, as a given industry goes through its life cycle of growth and decline, the central problem it faces changes from one of rapidly developing new technologies and products to the attainment of scale economies and production efficiencies in a climate of relatively stable markets and technology. The focus of the enterprises in the industry turns from the entrepreneurial task of carving out a major new market or developing a major new technology to the managerial task of building a large organization capable of producing at the lowest possible unit costs. In short, mature enterprises lose their facility to be entrepreneurial.

Since corporations facing market saturation are frequently unable to create their own new product markets, they often solve their problem by simply acquiring existing businesses that are experiencing rapid growth. The problem with this approach for regions in which such corporations are based is that the businesses being acquired are usually located in other regions that are in the early stages of the expansion phase of their long waves. Thus corporations shift capital out of regions experiencing economic stagnation and into regions experiencing relatively rapid growth, thereby further accentuating the existing pattern of uneven growth.

The slow-growth phase of a regional long wave creates substantial economic disruption for the region involved. A partial list of problems associated with regional economic stagnation would include high levels of unemployment, the permanent displacement of workers from high-paying jobs in mature industries, increased burdens on unemployment insurance and welfare programs, declining tax revenues, an increase in the bankruptcy rate, declining property values, and increased crime rates. Can the slow-growth phase of the regional long wave be mitigated through institutional reform? Or must regions simply accept their fate and suffer through a period of stagnation before new industries develop?

The central proposition in the final chapter of this book is that regions do not have to accept their fate; they can short-circuit the regional long wave through institutional reform. The root cause of the long wave can be traced to fundamental flaws in the modern corporation. On the one hand, the large bureaucratic corporation has great difficulty undertaking revolutionary innovations that lead to the creation of new industries, while on the other hand it has no responsibility to maintain employment opportunities for its existing employees or expand employment opportunities in the regions where it is located. The legal responsibility of the corporation is to its stockholders, not to its employees. If the maximizing of profits dictates that existing employees be laid off and existing production facilities shut down, then corporations will do so as a matter of responsibility to shareholders.

Consequently, to short-circuit the long wave, a business institutional arrangement is needed that is entrepreneurial and responsible to its employees, and has strong ties to a given region. The task of chapters 3–5 is to show that producer cooperatives, in association with a cooperative financial institution, fill the bill. Producer cooperatives are owned and democratically controlled by their employees. The primary responsibility of the producer cooperative will thus be to maintain economic opportunities for its employees, and it will have a strong incentive to develop new products when old products are faced with market saturation. The shifting of capital from a declining to a growing region through acquisitions will not be an option available to a producer cooperative. Since a producer cooperative serves a specific group of employees in a given locality, it will be tied to a given region. A properly structured cooperative financial institution required to invest only in associated producer cooperatives can facilitate the new business formation process by providing finance capital as well as technical assistance to individuals and groups that want to start new cooperative enterprises. Such an institution can thus accelerate the new business formation process and shorten the slow-growth phase of the long wave. Such an institution can also assist existing cooperatives faced with market saturation in seeking out new high-growth product lines.

The first step in the chapters that follow will be to set out in detail the theory of the regional long wave. The task of Chapter 3 will be to provide empirical support for the regional long wave. In Chapter 4 the theoretical underpinnings of the cooperative alternative will be set out and the advantages of cooperatives for regional development will be considered. Attention will also be given to the basic problems that cooperatives face in a market economy and the necessary institutional innovations needed to overcome those problems. Chapter 5 will be devoted to an evaluation of the historical experience of cooperatives, while Chapter 6 will consider exactly how a cooperative economic sector can be created at the regional level in this country.

NOTES

1.	The evidence for these propositions will be provided in Chapter 3.

2.	For an excellent summary and analysis of long-wave theory, see Van Duijn 1983.

3.	The infrastructural investment cycle will be presented here in a somewhat simplified form. For a treatment of the details and subtleties of infrastructure investment cycles, see ibid., 112–28.

4.	The infrastructure long wave described here results in large measure from the long life of infrastructure capital facilities. Forrester (of systems dynamics fame) has developed a long-wave theory based on capital facilities that have a relatively short life span (ibid., 147–92).

5.	For empirical evidence supporting this theory of the long wave, see ibid.

2

LONG WAVES AND UNEVEN REGIONAL GROWTH: THEORY

Historical studies reveal that economic growth in the United States has always been an uneven affair. Over any given period of time, some regions experience rapid economic growth while others face economic stagnation. The phenomenon of uneven growth has become increasingly apparent in the 1970s and 1980s, with the dramatic losses of manufacturing employment in the industrial states of the East and Midwest, and the boom in economic activity taking place in the southern rim states.

The conventional view of this process is that corporations are moving production facilities away from the industrial states in order to avoid unions, high wages, high taxes, and extensive government regulation (Bluestone & Harrison 1982, 111–90). In many cases, corporations are avoiding the United States entirely and are choosing to locate in low-wage Third World countries. This practice has become increasingly feasible with rapid improvements in communications and transportation technologies.

Pathbreaking empirical work by David L. Birch (1979) on regional employment growth and decline has begun to illuminate the process of uneven development more clearly and to suggest that the conventional view is at best incomplete. In theory, a given region will gain employment from work force expansions in existing business establishments, and the movement of existing business establishments

Portions of this chapter appeared in the *Southern Economic Journal,* October 1986, under the title "Long Waves and Uneven Regional Growth." Reprinted by permission.

from other regions, and will lose employment from work force contractions in existing business establishments, the shutdown of existing business establishments, and the movement of existing business
establishments to other regions. Contrary to popular opinion, the
movement of business establishments from one region to another accounts for a very small percentage of employment gains and losses in
the United States. In addition, the rate of employment loss from facility shutdowns and work force reductions differs little from one region to another (Birch 1979, 20–42).

These conclusions suggest that emphasis on plant shutdowns
and contractions in explaining uneven development between regions
is misplaced. The critical difference between regions is the rate of employment gain from work force expansions in existing business establishments and the creation of new business establishments. Surprisingly, all regions of the country suffer substantial employment losses
each year from plant shutdowns and work force reductions. Regions
that experience relatively high growth rates in net employment,
however, are characterized by significantly higher rates of employment gains from the creation of new business establishments and
work force expansions in existing establishments than are regions of
the country experiencing low rates of net employment growth. In
other words, the key to regional economic growth is the creation of
new employment through the establishment of new businesses and
the expansion of existing businesses rather than through a defensive
strategy of preventing the decline of existing businesses. Another remarkable finding of this research is that from 75 to 80 percent of all
new jobs created over the period 1974–76 occurred in firms that were
less than four years old (Birch 1979, 32). It is the relatively new entrepreneurial venture that is responsible for the bulk of employment creation in this country rather than the long-established large corporation. These empirical findings clearly suggest the need for an alternative conception of the uneven development process that focuses on
the process of creating new businesses rather than on the decline of
aging enterprises.

The purpose of this book is to suggest that uneven regional development is a manifestation of regional long waves of economic
growth and decline, and that disparities between regions in such
things as unionization, labor costs, and taxes are simply the result of
different regions being at different phases of development in their respective long waves. The essence of the view to be presented in the fol-

lowing pages is that regions experience long periods of sustained rapid economic growth followed by relatively lengthy periods of slow economic growth or economic decline. The growth retardation stage of the long wave sets up the conditions for an eventual economic recovery and a return to a more rapid rate of growth. The present chapter will be devoted to presenting the theoretical underpinnings of regional long waves; supporting empirical evidence will be presented in Chapter 3.

LONG WAVES AND INDUSTRIAL LIFE CYCLES

Historical studies have established the existence of industrial life cycles. According to the empirical investigations of Arthur Burns, new industries experience a period of rapid growth after an initial phase of incubation and, as a consequence of competition from still newer industries, eventually face a retardation in growth or, in some instances, absolute decline (Burns 1934, 48–169). The existence of industrial cycles can be explained by the Schumpeterian concept of competition involving a constant struggle in the marketplace between entrepreneurs to gain a monopoly position in a new commodity, a new technology, a new source of supply, or a new type of organization (Schumpeter 1950, 83). Any competitive edge gained in this struggle is ultimately eroded by the competition of still newer marketplace innovations. The dynamics of capital accumulation thus involve a constantly changing mix of products, technologies, sources of supply, and forms of business organization, and new industries periodically emerge to replace old industries as growth leaders in the economy. The early stages of the industrial life cycle are generally characterized by rapid technological change requiring relatively flexible, labor-intensive production processes, while the later stages involve a stabilizing of technology, saturation of product markets, and increasing concern with cutting unit production costs through the attainment of scale economies.[1]

The possible connection between the industrial life cycle, and the growth and decline of regions is fairly obvious. The growth of a region will be stimulated by the presence of industries in the rapid-growth phase of the life cycle, and retarded by the presence of industries in the slow-growth or decline phase of the life cycle. If a given region has an appropriate, stable balance of old and new industries, clearly it need not experience a decline in its aggregate rate of growth.

However, there is empirical evidence suggesting that localities and regions with aging industries suffer through relatively lengthy periods of time without developing substantial economic activity in new, rapid-growth industries.[2] If this is in fact the case, there must exist important barriers in such regions to the formation of new industries.

New industries are generally created by new businesses. Only rarely do existing large enterprises in already established industries become the driving force for the creation of entirely new industries.[3] The development of new industries in a given region thus hinges on the formation of new businesses. The creation of successful new businesses that can form the basis for new industries is a stochastic process. Many new businesses are formed, but only a few are selected by the marketplace for success. Businesses that are successful are either adopted by the marketplace—they happen to produce a commodity that is in demand—or they adapt to the marketplace by developing a product that is in demand (Alchain). In general, the greater the rate of new business formation in a region, the greater the likelihood that businesses will be selected for success and will serve as the basis for the development of new industries.

IMPEDIMENTS TO NEW BUSINESS CREATION

Consequently, the central issue is this: Why are there impediments to the formation of new businesses in older regions with mature industries? An important potential barrier to the formation of new businesses in regions that have already experienced industrial development is a substantial number of large, older businesses that are nearing the end of the rapid-growth phase of their life cycle. Such businesses have turned from an earlier entrepreneurial orientation to a managerial orientation. As already noted, in the early stages of an industry's life cycle, technologies and products will be in a constant state of flux and change. This means that businesses must maintain flexibility in order to meet such changes, and flexibility and the ability to innovate rapidly are the hallmark of the entrepreneurial enterprise. Once an industry matures and technology stabilizes, production runs will lengthen and the achievement of scale economies will become important. The nature of the problem faced by firms in such an industry will shift from the need for flexibility to the need to successfully manage production on a large scale in an environment of relative technological stability. The focus will shift from entrepreneurship to management.

Why would the presence of a substantial number of managerially oriented enterprises in a given region limit the extent of new business formation and creation of new industries? Managerial enterprises are less concerned with the creation of new products and technologies that differ significantly from the old than they are with the successful large-scale production of existing products. Individuals who work for such enterprises consequently gain skills in the management of a large, stable business organization, not skills in the creation and marketing of revolutionary new products and technologies, and in the operating of flexible enterprises capable of carrying out rapid innovation. Large, managerially oriented enterprises thus train managers, not entrepreneurs who would be capable of starting new businesses.

In addition, mature, managerially oriented enterprises provide relatively secure, well-paying opportunities for individuals who might otherwise start new businesses. Those who have the potential for entrepreneurial activity may well be attracted to the easy life of the large, established corporation rather than to the risk and long hours associated with the starting of a new business.

The presence of large, mature enterprises could also place a limit on the availability of venture capital for new businesses. Those who have successfully accumulated wealth in mature businesses are unlikely to take the risk associated with investing in new businesses when the old have served them so well. Not only capital, but other inputs as well, will flow to the stable opportunities provided by mature enterprises. Labor will prefer employment in the larger, stable enterprises to those that are new and unstable. Suppliers of business services and other inputs will prefer the large-volume contracts offered by the larger enterprises to the small orders provided by new businesses.

THE RECOVERY PROCESS

Once employment opportunities begin to decline in mature industries, the prospects for new business formation begin to change. Managerial opportunities in mature enterprises will begin to disappear. Those with business skills who choose not to migrate to more dynamic regions will increasingly turn to the formation of new businesses. In addition, capital, labor, and other inputs that were historically attracted to local mature industries will now more likely flow to new local businesses with the disappearance of the old opportunities. The fundamental problem is that a lengthy incubation period is often required before new businesses that manage to survive grow to the point where they become major employers.[4] Since business survival may require learning from the mistakes of others, considerable time may pass before ultimate survivors emerge in a given industry. In the meantime, an older region with mature industries in a state of decline will experience slow economic growth and the social problems associated with inadequate employment opportunities.[5] Eventually new industries will emerge and regional growth will recover, but the time lapse between the growth phase of one wave of expansion and that of another could well be lengthy.

BARRIERS TO CORPORATE INNOVATION

Before considering empirical evidence supporting the existence of regional long waves, one issue remains to be resolved. Why don't mature, large corporations in older regions develop new products and new technologies that can serve as the basis for new industries?

As already noted, the fundamental problem of large, mature enterprises is to organize production on a large scale. In theory, this could be accomplished in two ways. Production could be organized on a highly decentralized basis, with considerable autonomy and responsibility being given to individual employees and groups of employees. While this approach could lead to high levels of productive efficiency, it would give employees a considerable monopoly over knowledge of the production process, and they could use this monopoly to extract higher income levels and better working conditions from top management and owners of the enterprise.[6] This in turn would reduce profitability. The alternative is to organize production in a way that uses division of labor and bureaucratic methods of management.[7] Through a division of labor, the extent of idiosyncratic knowledge gained by any individual employee or group of employees can be limited.[8] Production knowledge can be retained to a large extent by top management in the form of formalized production procedures. In such a production scheme, the activities and responsibilities of each and every individual are carefully spelled out in elaborate job descriptions, and a managerial hierarchy is carefully crafted to monitor the activities of each and every employee (Edwards 1979, 130–62). The bargaining power of individual employees and small groups of employees is thus reduced, thereby increasing enterprise profits.

The problem with the bureaucratic form of management is that it diminishes the ability of large enterprises to undertake substantial innovation. Employee autonomy, and management and organizational flexibility are required for significant innovation.[9] Bureaucratic procedures preclude autonomy and inhibit flexibility. While large corporations are capable of undertaking incremental innovations where the division of labor can be readily applied to the process of innovation, revolutionary innovations generally depend on the creativity of individuals or small groups of individuals who have the freedom to determine their own actions and activities. If such groups within a large corporation are given autonomy, they will likely pursue activities beneficial to themselves rather than to the enterprise as a whole, unless they feel some extraordinary bond of solidarity with the enterprise. Even if revolutionary innovations are forthcoming within an enterprise, they may not survive approval through a chain of command that is likely to contain at least one decision maker who sees a loss of authority resulting from the project or is fearful of taking the necessary risks involved (Scherer 1980, 414). Empiricial evidence suggests that very large corporations are only infrequently the source of major innovations (Scherer 1980, 412–22). Of course there are exceptions. Some older enterprises are sufficiently flexible to move into new product lines. Normally, however, they will not do this until their traditional business activity is sufficiently threatened, and considerable time may well pass, while they are developing their new products and technologies, before they again become major employers in the local economy.[10]

CONCLUSION

The central conclusion of the above theory is that uneven development between different regions of the country can be attributed to a long-wave process. A given region historically experiences a lengthy period of relatively rapid economic growth that is followed by a lengthy period of relatively poor economic growth. The period of poor growth establishes the conditions for a recovery to higher rates of growth. The central problem of this phenomenon is the economic displacement and suffering that result during the period of poor economic growth. A principal thesis of this book is that major institutional change is needed to smooth out the long wave and to reduce the hardships that result from inadequate economic growth.

NOTES

1. For a good description of the industrial life cycle and its application to the computer industry, see Wilson, Ashton & Egan 1980, 11–18. What is called the industrial life cycle here is often referred to as the product life cycle.

2. Watkins (1980) points out that older cities, concentrated primarily in the eastern United States, did not alter their industrial mix very much in the first part of the century and, consequently, did not capture new high-growth industries, such as rubber products and automotive equipment. These industries concentrated instead in the younger cities of the Midwest. Norton and Rees (1979) argue that the new science-based industries in recent years have increasingly located outside the old industrial belt, in the peripheral states of the South and West.

3. For example, in the semiconductor industry none of the large corporations that produced vacuum tubes were successful in semiconductor production (Wilson, Ashton & Egan 1980, 5, 22).

4. There are no studies that I know of on the length of this incubation process. One firm in the computer industry, Wang Laboratories, was founded in 1951 but did not exceed $1 million in revenue until 1964. Its revenues reached $100 million in 1977 and $2 billion in 1984 (Wessell 1984). On the other hand, Texas Instruments, in the semiconductor industry, grew rather rapidly soon after its founding (Wilson, Ashton & Egan, 16).

5. For an analysis of economic and social problems associated with regional decline, see Bluestone & Harrison 1982.

6. Corporations have engaged in experiments with increasing worker autonomy, experiments that have almost invariably resulted in increased productivity levels (Jenkins 1973, Ch. 12). Nonetheless, these experiments have often been canceled, and worker autonomy has not been widely adopted in U.S. industry (Edwards 1979, 155–57). This supports the view that employee autonomy alters the bargaining relationship between management and employees. One might argue that if efficiency gains result from employee autonomy, a contract between management and employees could be written requiring that those efficiency gains be shared by both parties. The problem is that management cannot always enforce such a contract adequately. Suppose that after worker autonomy is established and workers gain idiosyncratic knowledge of the production process, workers undertake a wildcat strike for higher pay. Management could go to court to have the contract enforced, but this would be self-defeating if the workers still refused to return to the job. Ultimately, management would have to deal with the workers' new demands. If the new system of production under worker autonomy involved a substantial capital outlay, returning to the old system of production may no longer be a feasible option for management.

7. For a historical analysis of the emergence of bureaucracy as a means for controlling the activities of employees, see ibid., 130–62.

8. Williamson was one of the first to suggest that workers in production organizations would develop idiosyncratic knowledge that they could, in theory, refuse to pass on to others. This would give them bargaining power relative to management, since such workers would be difficult to replace as a consequence of their monopoly of knowledge needed to carry out production. Williamson suggests further that the problem of worker bargaining power is avoided through the development of job ladders and the attachment of wage rates to jobs rather than to individuals, thus removing wages as a subject of bargaining between workers and managers. The problem with Williamson's argument is that workers will still be able, in effect, to bargain over other issues, such as promotions, working conditions, and days off. The alternative is to reduce the amount of idiosyncratic knowledge a worker can gain by employing an extensive division of labor and carefully specifying, through job descriptions, how each and every production task is to be carried out (Booth 1985).

9. Managerial and organizational flexibility were key elements in fostering high levels of innovation in the semiconductor industry during its rapid-growth phase (Wilson, Ashton & Egan 1980, 50–56).

10. This was the case with at least one Milwaukee corporation. After suffering decline in its traditional product lines for a number of years, Rexnord Incorporated has begun to move into new, high-growth product lines involving more sophisticated technology (Helyar 1984).

3

REGIONAL LONG WAVES:
HISTORICAL EVIDENCE

Is there any empirical evidence that regional long waves of development like those described above exist in practice? Do developed regions of the country suffer declining relative growth rates as they age, and subsequently experience a surge in new business formation and eventually a recovery in economic growth? Is the rate of new business formation determined by the industrial life cycle described above, or do more conventional variables, such as unionization, labor supply, and the magnitude of local taxes, influence new business formation? These are the central issues to be addressed in the pages to follow.

UNEVEN GROWTH IN MANUFACTURING

By the turn of the 20th century, two key regions of the country had experienced substantial industrial and economic development. As can be seen in Table 3.1, a belt of heavily industrialized states had emerged, beginning with Massachusetts in New England and continuing through Rhode Island, Connecticut, New York, New Jersey, Pennsylvania, Ohio, Indiana, Michigan, Illinois, and Wisconsin. These eleven states contained 71 percent of all manufacturing employment in the country in 1900. Western states in this industrial belt developed later than the eastern states. Consequently the belt is divided into two segments, one containing Massachusetts, Rhode Island,

Portions of this chapter have appeared in the *Southern Economic Journal,* October 1986, under the title "Long Waves and Uneven Regional Growth." Reprinted by permission.

Connecticut, New York, New Jersey, and Pennsylvania, and the other containing Ohio, Indiana, Michigan, Illinois, and Wisconsin.

Manufacturing employment growth rates for eastern and western industrial states relative to the aggregate U.S. manufacturing employment growth rates for the period 1860–1981 are presented in Table 3.2. The figure presented is the regional employment growth rate minus the growth rate for the United States as a whole. The growth rate of the eastern industrial states is below the national growth rate for each census period from 1880 to 1981. The growth rate of the western industrial states is at or above the national growth rate from 1860 to 1930 and thereafter is below it. Prior to 1920 employment growth in the eastern states was still substantial in an absolute sense because of the rapid growth in U.S. employment in general. From 1920 on, however, the eastern states have increasingly experienced periods of manufacturing employment decline. By 1981 the employment level of the eastern states was only 2.2 percent above the 1920 figure and had fallen 6.9 percent below the 1947 figure (U.S. Bureau of the Census 1920, 1947, 1981). After World War II the growth rate of the western industrial states was generally above that of the eastern states, except for the final period considered, 1977–81. In this period the eastern industrial states experienced a recovery in growth up to within 2 percent of the national rate, while the western industrial states fell 12 percent behind the national growth rate.

In terms of long-wave analysis, the eastern industrial states have experienced relatively poor employment growth in manufacturing for a considerable time and may be entering a recovery phase involving higher rates of growth. On the other hand, the western industrial states have experienced poor or negative growth only in the past few decades and appear still to be in the decline phase of a long wave. If long waves in regional growth exist, their life span appears to be lengthy, possibly a full century. While the data in Table 3.2 are suggestive, to prove the existence of regional long waves with certainty will require a more extensive historical experience. Many regions in this country are still in the early stages of their rapid-growth phase, and it remains to be seen whether they will follow the historical pattern experienced in the industrial East or Midwest.

As suggested by the data in Table 3.3, many states in the South, Southwest, and West have had relative growth rates in manufacturing above those experienced in the East and Midwest since the 1940s. The locus of manufacturing growth clearly has shifted to regions of

TABLE 3.1
**Manufacturing Employ-
ment, 1900**

State	Employment
Maine	85646
New Hampshire	77739
Vermont	35801
Massachusetts	557233
Rhode Island	107702
Connecticut	196056
New York	1012290
New Jersey	274303
Pennsylvania	840109
Ohio	412496
Indiana	187560
Illinois	480643
Michigan	194893
Wisconsin	170083
Minnesota	96806
Iowa	80826
Missouri	169534
North Dakota	3818
South Dakota	5164
Nebraska	33060
Kansas	47925
Maryland	127033
Virginia	86321
West Virginia	40213
North Carolina	82044
South Carolina	53748
Georgia	96873
Florida	38484
Kentucky	79274
Tennessee	63995
Alabama	62176
Mississippi	33382
Arkansas	33901
Louisiana	50915
Oklahoma	3255
Texas	65707
Montana	11832
Idaho	2243
Wyoming	2711
Colorado	30444
New Mexico	3153
Arizona	3787
Utah	885
Nevada	887
Washington	40154
Oregon	22115
California	113155

Source: U.S. Bureau of the Census, 1900.

TABLE 3.2
Relative Manufacturing Employment Growth Rates

Time Period	1800–1870	1870–1880	1880–1890	1890–1900	1900–1910	1910–1920	1920–1930	1930–1940	1947–1954	1954–1967	1967–1972	1972–1977	1977–1981
1. Industrial Belt Eastern Segment	-15.4	2.0	-20.7	-7.0	-3.2	-7.8	-8.9	-3.6	-6.8	-16.9	-9.2	-9.0	-2.0
2. Industrial Belt Western Segment	88.0	4.7	27.8	3.2	.7	20.7	7.5	-2.0	-6.1	-7.7	-2.7	-2.2	-12.0
3. U.S. Manufacturing Employment Growth Rate	56.0	33.0	72.0	32.6	22.9	40.8	-4.4	-7.2	12.6	10.7	-1.5	3.0	4.0

Notes: This rate is defined as the percentage change in manufacturing employment for the region minus the percentage change in manufacturing employment for the United States as a whole.

Source: U.S. Bureau of the Census 1860–1940, 1954–1983.

TABLE 3.3
Relative Manufacturing Employment Growth Rates

State	1947-1954	1954-1967	1967-1972	1972-1977	1977-1981
Maine	-7.7	-14.0	-8.4	0.0	7.7
New Hampshire	-9.6	3.7	-3.7	2.6	12.8
Vermont	-9.4	-.3	-12.5	12.5	15.1
Massachusetts	-17.1	-15.6	-11.8	-4.0	8.9
Rhode Island	-27.5	-22.1	-1.8	2.9	-2.4
Connecticut	-7.4	-5.8	-15.0	.3	6.4
New York	.4	-23.6	-11.5	-13.1	-4.5
New Jersey	-2.6	-11.2	-3.6	-9.9	-2.1
Pennsylvania	-10.3	-14.4	-7.0	-9.2	-6.8
Ohio	-4.4	-11.7	-2.1	-4.1	-12.4
Indiana	-5.3	1.0	.7	-2.7	-12.9
Illinois	-9.4	-5.4	-5.0	-4.5	-9.9
Michigan	-4.0	-12.4	-3.6	-4.7	-16.5
Wisconsin	-7.2	-3.1	-.6	3.8	-5.3
Minnesota	3.5	23.8	2.1	6.9	8.3
Iowa	4.2	8.3	4.4	8.1	-5.6
Missouri	4.0	-1.4	-2.5	-3.2	-4.6
North Dakota	2.4	13.6	26.5	37.0	3.1
South Dakota	4.3	13.6	7.8	32.3	13.4
Nebraska	12.8	10.8	11.9	32.5	4.0
Kansas	62.9	-9.8	-3.3	19.6	7.9
Maryland	-1.0	-6.7	-9.6	-7.7	-4.4
Virginia	-.4	20.2	11.8	2.3	0.1
West Virginia	-16.8	-18.1	-.9	-6.3	-10.8
North Carolina	1.4	28.1	17.2	-1.8	3.4
South Carolina	4.0	18.5	15.0	5.4	-2.3
Georgia	8.6	19.9	12.1	.6	4.6
Florida	45.0	110.1	21.9	1.4	25.1
Kentucky	4.0	29.3	16.6	4.3	-8.0
Tennessee	8.0	36.9	13.2	1.9	-3.6
Alabama	-5.8	11.7	13.3	2.6	-2.5
Mississippi	6.1	56.1	26.5	6.5	12.9
Arkansas	8.3	62.6	27.5	5.8	-4.0
Louisiana	-3.1	-5.9	10.0	5.9	2.7
Oklahoma	48.0	12.9	22.7	11.7	21.0
Texas	28.5	37.3	13.4	17.4	16.5
Montana	5.5	-14.4	6.5	11.3	-8.2
Idaho	23.4	41.2	17.7	17.9	-7.8
Wyoming	-5.5	-19.7	18.2	25.6	18.2
Colorado	5.8	42.8	29.4	12.0	18.9
New Mexico	85.0	-6.3	42.8	17.8	13.2
Arizona	70.6	176.5	23.6	15.1	36.5
Utah	9.8	37.0	22.8	19.8	27.4
Nevada	112.4	-3.0	44.4	47.0	16.0
Washington	21.8	20.0	-15.1	14.3	10.7
Oregon	15.3	1.0	11.3	9.8	-3.0
California	46.0	30.7	-.9	12.3	12.4

Source: U.S. Bureau of the Census 1954-83.

the country that did not have much manufacturing develpment prior
to World War II and thus are not burdened with aging, declining industries. The growth of these states required that certain necessary
conditions be satisfied, such as the development of transportation facilities and public works. With federal government assistance, public
facilities were developed in the southern rim states as part of a larger
effort to prevent a return to the Great Depression of the 1930s through
Keynesian-inspired public expenditures (Watkins 1980, 232–33). Since
these states lacked major established industries, ambitious individuals
desiring to achieve positions of wealth would have to start new businesses, and economic logic suggests that new, rapid-growth industries
would be the preferred choice. Thus the newer industries, such as
aerospace, semiconductors, and computers, concentrated heavily in
states outside the industrial belt. An important exception is the concentration of part of the computer industry in eastern states (Hekman
1980). As we will see, the East experienced a surge in new business formation after World War II and after suffering through many years of
relatively slow economic growth.

THE LONG WAVE AND NEW BUSINESS FORMATION

The theory presented in Chapter 2 suggests that retardation of regional growth will set the stage for an acceleration of new business formation. Statistics on new business formation are not readily available
for any lengthy period of time. While not all new business formations
involve new incorporations, a reasonable assumption is that new
incorporations will be positively related to the rate of new business formation. Statistics are available from Dun & Bradstreet on the number
of new incorporations by state from 1948 on (Dun & Bradstreet
1950–82).

The data in Table 3.4 indicate that incorporations per thousand
population have clearly been above the national figure in the eastern
segment of the industrial belt since 1950, while they have been well below the national figure in the western segment of the industrial belt.[1]
The higher level of new incorporations in the eastern states is consis-
tent with the view presented above that a region with a history of slow
economic growth will have a higher-than-normal rate of new business
formation. The low level of new business formation in the western segment of the industrial belt suggests that the retardation of growth in
the midwestern region has not yet been of sufficient duration to stimulate new business formation.

TABLE 3.4
Average Annual Number of Incorporations per Thousand Population

		1950–59	1960–68	1969–76	1977–82
1.	Industrial Belt: Eastern Segment	1.119	1.277	1.830	2.033
2.	Industrial Belt: Western Segment	.613	.802	1.059	1.424
3.	United States	.770	1.041	1.460	1.964

Sources: The Dun & Bradstreet Corporation, Economic Analysis Department, 1950–82; U.S. Bureau of the Census, 1954–83.

The individual state data presented in Table 3.5 also support the proposition that the rate of new incorporations is greater at the eastern end of the industrial belt than at the western end. Is the rate of new incorporations significantly greater in a statistical sense at the eastern end of the industrial belt? Are there other variables that could explain variations in the rate of new incorporations? These questions are addressed in the regression results of Table 3.6.

The analysis presented in Table 3.6 supports the conclusion that the rate of new incorporations was indeed significantly greater at the eastern end of the industrial belt over the period 1950–82. Across a sample of 47 states in 4 regressions with the rate of new incorporations as the dependant variable, a dummy variable on the six states at the eastern end of the industrial belt is statistically significant and positive. On the other hand, the dummy variable for states at the western end of the industrial belt was statistically insignificant. Each dummy variable can be viewed as a proxy for the age of its region's long wave of development. The eastern segment of the industrial belt is farthest along in its cycle, while the western segment is at an earlier stage of its long wave. These results and the data presented above on relative growth rates suggest that the eastern end of the industrial belt has suffered retardation of growth for a period of time sufficient to stimulate higher levels of new business formation, while the western end has only just begun to experience a significant reduction in relative growth.

TABLE 3.5
Average Annual Incorporations per Thousand Population

State	1950-59	1960-68	1969-76	1977-82
Maine	.489	.702	1.150	1.348
New Hampshire	.711	1.086	1.410	1.341
Vermont	.553	1.025	1.679	2.098
Massachusetts	.794	1.000	1.400	1.634
Rhode Island	1.132	1.332	1.784	2.028
Connecticut	.904	1.084	1.345	1.827
New York	1.657	2.036	2.558	2.715
New Jersey	1.411	1.540	2.137	2.496
Pennsylvania	.383	.591	.848	.985
Ohio	.786	.928	1.119	1.203
Indiana	.445	.654	1.025	1.252
Illinois	.641	.842	1.045	1.792
Michigan	.509	.691	1.046	1.475
Wisconsin	.526	.794	1.017	1.141
Minnesota	.497	.725	1.234	1.515
Iowa	.280	.695	1.161	1.507
Missouri	.540	.852	1.290	1.511
North Dakota	.332	.534	.916	1.351
South Dakota	.354	.999	.978	1.155
Nebraska	.417	.814	1.330	1.622
Kansas	.398	.642	1.175	1.618
Maryland	.911	1.299	1.492	1.861
Virginia	.497	.796	1.207	1.755
West Virginia	.360	.539	.845	1.233
North Carolina	.398	.653	1.082	1.295
South Carolina	.382	.620	.950	1.141
Georgia	.505	.875	1.514	1.870
Florida	1.881	2.040	2.704	4.138
Kentucky	.355	.619	1.023	1.225
Tennessee	.406	.680	1.018	1.269
Alabama	.307	.591	.847	.962
Mississippi	.261	.619	1.008	1.290
Arkansas	.324	.798	1.216	1.417
Louisiana	.513	1.029	1.390	2.265
Oklahoma	.578	.903	1.216	1.908
Texas	.571	.863	1.204	2.134
Montana	.612	.755	1.262	1.713
Idaho	.629	.886	1.360	1.667
Wyoming	.843	1.207	1.725	2.467
Colorado	.984	1.437	2.031	2.917
New Mexico	.579	.786	1.271	1.631
Arizona	1.278	1.442	1.898	2.606
Utah	.722	1.211	1.711	2.186
Nevada	4.411	4.455	5.194	6.791
Washington	.608	.819	1.167	1.703
Oregon	.648	1.013	1.418	2.073
California	.927	.831	1.085	1.881

Source: The Dun & Bradstreet Corporation, Economic Analysis Department, 1950–82; U.S. Bureau of the Census, 1954–83.

TABLE 3.6.
The Determinants of the New Incorporation Rate

Independent Variables	Dependent Variable: Incorporations Per Thousand Population			
	(1) 1950–59	(2) 1960–68	(3) 1969–76	(4) 1976–82
Eastern Segment Industrial Belt Dummy Variable	4.768* (2.02)	4.113* (2.51)	5.810* (2.47)	7.081* (2.35)
Western Segment Industrial Belt Dummy Variable	-.776 (-.32)	-.84 (-.49)	-1.983 (-.84)	1.230 (.41)
Percent Change Population	25.284* (5.54)	45.076* (9.15)	40.241* (6.70)	65.633* (5.93)
Tax Effort	.035 (.65)	.011 (.27)	.008 (.18)	.003 (.05)
Percent Work Force Unionized		.006 (.13)	.132 (1.43)	.031 (.22)
Unemployment Rate		-.226 (-.36)	-.172 (-.29)	.040 (.05)
Defense Procurement Expenditures Per Capita		-13.767* (-2.02)	-11.479 (-1.73)	-2.767 (-.49)
Intercept		4.038 (.98)	4.590 (1.12)	5.972 (1.05)
Statistics				
R^2	.45	.71	.59	.52
F	8.406	13.457	7.866	6.092

Notes: The figures in parentheses are t statistics; an asterisk indicates that the coefficient is significantly greater than zero at the five percent level or less.

The tax effort variable is the ratio of state and local taxes to the total state and local revenue capacity. This is a crude measure of the aggregate tax burden on a state's population and businesses. Other variables were tried, such as corporate and personal income tax effort, with statistically insignificant results.

Population growth rate was lagged two years in each regression.

Data from the midpoint or years close to the midpoint of the time period for each regression were used for independent variables other than the population growth rate and the regional dummy variables. Midpoint data best reflect conditions over the period involved (rather than starting point data).

Delaware is omitted from the sample because of laws that provide special inducements to businesses to incorporate there.

For the period 1950–59 data were not available for the percent of the work force unionized, the unemployment rate, and defense procurement expenditures per capita.

Sources: New incorporation data, Dun & Bradstreet 1950–82; tax effort variable, U.S. Advisory Commission on Intergovernmental Relations 1962, 1983; all other data, U.S. Bureau of the Census 1954–83.

Other variables, of course, are likely to have an influence on the rate of new incorporations. New incorporations reflect the formation of new businesses to serve national and international markets as well as new businesses to serve local markets. The latter component is likely to be related to the growth rate of local population. This hypothesis is supported in Table 3.6 by the statistically significant positive regression coefficients on the lagged rate of population growth in the regression equations.

As noted in Chapter 2, conventional arguments suggest that differences in economic growth rates across regions can be explained by differences in the availability of labor, the extent of unionization, and the level of local taxes. Such differences can be explained as a consequence of different states being at different phases of their long waves of growth and decline. A state that has a long history of industrial development is also likely to have a more extensive union movement. Since the building of a union movement is a time-consuming process, states with longer histories of industrial development will have higher rates of unionization among their workers.[2]

TABLE 3.7.
Unionization and Tax Effort

State	Percent of Work Force Unionized 1980	Tax Effort 1981
Massachusetts	24.9	134.0
Rhode Island	28.4	129.9
Connnecticut	22.9	102.7
New York	38.7	111.7
New Jersey	25.6	104.8
Pennsylvania	34.6	104.8
Ohio	31.5	88.7
Indiana	30.4	105.0
Illinois	30.6	116.1
Michigan	37.4	120.3
Wisconsin	28.6	120.3
US	25.2	100.0

Sources: U.S. Bureau of the Census 1981–83; U.S. Advisory Commission on Intergovernmental Relations 1983.

The data on unionization presented in Table 3.7 indicate that unionization is somewhat higher in the industrial belt than in other regions of the country. However, the regression analysis of Table 3.6 suggests that the extent of unionization has no perceptible effect on the rate of new incorporations. The explanation for this result may be that unionization is not readily transferable from old to new industries, and, as a result, new businesses need not avoid locations that have high levels of unionization in order to avoid having a unionized work force. New industries with a maze of relatively small and unstable new firms will be difficult to organize.[3] Unions are more likely to appear in an industry when markets and technologies have stabilized and the long-term survivors have emerged.

In addition to unionization, other labor market variables could in theory have some impact on the rate of new business formation. Clearly, new businesses need to be able to attract new employees at a reasonable wage, and, in theory, location in a region with a higher rate of unemployment should ease that task. According to the statistical results in Table 3.6, however, unemployment does not have a significant effect on incorporation rates.

The level of local taxation also can be explained theoretically in terms of a region's long wave of development. Regions with mature industries are likely to have higher levels of local government expenditures and taxation. Industries require local government inputs in order to operate.[4] Industrial development increases the average income of the local work force, which demands higher levels of local government services as a result.[5] Industrial development also creates problems, such as periodic unemployment, environmental pollution, and inadequate health and safety conditions that local governments must deal with. Local government expenditures respond in part to the needs of special interest groups. As in the case of unions, the building of organized special interests takes time.[6] Consequently, older regions of the country are likely to have more interest groups capable of placing pressure on local governments for higher spending levels. The data on relative tax effort presented in Table 3.7 indicate that it tends to be higher than the U.S. average in the industrial belt. However, the regression results in Table 3.6 suggest that tax effort does not have any statistically significant effect on the rate of new incorporations. Local taxes do not impose that much of a burden

on new businesses, particularly in the early years when such businesses do not earn much income and therefore do not incur much in the
way of income taxes. Also, new businesses are not likely to own substantial amounts of taxable property. In general, local taxes are not a
significant part of total production costs for most firms (Kieschnick
1981b, 41–46).

The final variable considered in the regression equations presented in Table 3.6 is per capita defense procurement expenditures.
Since World War II defense spending on procurement has had a
significant impact on relatively new high-growth industries such as
aerospace, semiconductors, and computers (Bluestone, Jordan &
Sullivan 1981, 157–70; Fisher, McKie & Mancke 1983 1–64; Soma
1976, 1–32; Wilson, Ashton & Egan 1980, 141–78). The relative distribution of such expenditures could in theory influence the rate of new
business formation if such disbursements are affected by factors other than the relative merits of competitive bids, such as political influence. If disbursements are made on the basis of competitive bids,
they simply reflect the prior distribution of firms. Whatever the case in
practice, defense expenditures per capita do not have a statistically significant positive impact on the new incorporation rate. For regression
equation (2), defense expenditures are statistically significant, but the
sign is negative. A possible interpretation of this result is that defense
expenditures flow to the larger, established firms that are able to attract employees who might otherwise start businesses of their own.

To summarize conclusions reached thus far, the rate of new
business formation, as reflected in the rate of new incorporations, is
significantly higher in the eastern segment of the industrial belt than in
the rest of the country. This same area has suffered from a retardation
of growth in manufacturing since the turn of the 20th century, which
suggests that retardation of growth sets the stage for an eventual increase in the rate of new business formation. Apart from local population growth, other variables, such as unionization, the local tax burden, unemployment, and defense spending, have no statistically significant impact on incorporation rates. As can be observed in Table 3.5,
relatively high incorporation rates have been occurring not only in the
older states of the industrial East, but in a number of states in the South,
Southwest, and West. The latter collection of states thus appears to be
in the relatively early stages of a wave of economic growth, while the
eastern states appear to be in a recovery phase after a lengthy period of
relatively slow economic growth.

Some have argued that shifting patterns of regional development can be traced to the differential availability of technological knowledge from major research universities (Hekman 1980; Norton & Rees 1979). Access to such major research institutions as MIT and Stanford has been critical in the development of the computer industry in the Boston area and the semiconductor industry in and around San Jose, California, respectively. In recent years numerous research universities, including the University of Wisconsin, the University of Utah, and Washington State University, attempted to develop research parks in order to attract new industries that can utilize university research capability. This behavior suggests that unversities respond to the expressed needs for local economic development. In older regions of the country that have an aging industrial structure, the need for the creation of new industries will be expressed most vocally when a retardation of economic growth has set in. In younger regions this need will be part of a general hunger to achieve a level of economic well-being and status that equals or exceeds those of other parts of the country. Public and nonprofit institutions whose financial health is directly connected to the health of the region in which they are located thus respond to economic conditions associated with regional long waves. When a region is experiencing economic success and significant growth, such institutions will be relatively complacent. When a region is experiencing economic distress, or is hungering for an economic status yet to be achieved, such institutions will undertake concerted action to foster economic development. The difficulty with this sort of a response pattern is that the lag between the decision to undertake action and positive results may be substantial. If it is, then the region in question may suffer through a lengthy period of poor economic growth before recovery takes hold.

CONCLUSION

If the experience of the eastern segment of the industrial belt is representative of a regional long-wave process, then economic recovery in the western segment of the industrial belt will be stretched out over a relatively long period of time. One possible view of the regional long-wave process is that economic and political interest groups hindering economic growth must be weakened before a resurgence of economic growth can take place (Olson 1983). While this may have some impact on employment in aging established enterprises, there is no evidence that the creation of new businesses is significantly influenced by the level of unionization or by the level of local taxation. Instead, the principal barrier to new business formation in older regions is simply the existence of established industries that divert potential entrepreneurs and other resources from the new business formation process. The formation of new businesses needed to provide the basis for new high-growth industries thus occurs only with the decline of the old industries in a region, and the period during which employment destruction in the old industries overpowers employment creation in new industries can be lengthy. The central question to be addressed in the remaining chapters of this book is whether the growth retardation phase of the regional long wave can be short-circuited by undertaking major reform in business institutions.

NOTES

1.   The numbers in Table 3.4 were derived by summing total incorporations over each of the four periods, dividing by population, and then dividing by the number of years in the time period. The population figure used in each case was an average of the census population nearest the end points, except for the last period, where the 1980 population figure was used.

2.   As Mancur Olson has pointed out, it is irrational to organize or join a union because it is in a public good (Olson 1971). This increases the difficulty of organizing a union and stretches out the time required for a union movement to gain momentum. The passage of the National Labor Relations Act in the 1930s reduced the barriers to union organization by requiring representation elections but did not totally eliminate them. Someone must still take the initiative for organizing such an election, and given the nature of the public goods problem, it may not pay for a single worker to take on the task. Paid organizers from existing unions can ease this problem; however, unions have limited resources to devote to organizing efforts, so the growth of a union movement will still be spread out over time.

3.   One relatively new industry, computers, is heavily concentrated in Massachusetts, New York, Minnesota, and California, all of which have relatively high rates of unionization (Hekman 1980).

4.   For evidence that business activity has a positive effect on local government expenditures, see Booth 1978.

5.   One of the standard results of the public finance empirical literature is that family income has a positive effect on local government expenditures (Borcherding & Deacon 1972).

6.   Mancur Olson (1982) suggests that over time, interest groups will emerge in a rapidly growing area of the country, the South, and that such interest groups will ultimately limit economic growth. His analysis is essentially the same as that presented here.

4

THE COOPERATIVE ALTERNATIVE: THEORY

If a regional development indeed takes place in a long wave involving a lengthy period of relatively rapid growth followed by a lengthy period of relatively slow growth or even decline in employment, and if during slow-growth periods employment creation is inadequate to meet the demands for employment resulting from a growing work force, then regions will suffer significant unemployment problems for long periods of time. Since different regions will generally be at different points in their long-wave development cycle at any moment in time, the degree of suffering from unemployment will be unevenly spread across regions. The extraordinarily high unemployment rates in the New England region between the end of World War II and the late 1970s have resulted from a long-wave pattern of development. Only with a recovery in its relative growth rate in the late 1970s have New England's unemployment rates fallen below national levels. Since the early 1980s the Midwest appears to have taken over the position as the country's laggard region, with declining relative growth rates and rising relative unemployment rates.

The social costs of regional slow growth and unemployment have been carefully described elsewhere and need not be considered in great detail here (Bluestone & Harrison 1982, 49–107). Workers who become unemployed as a result of plant shutdowns or work force reductions suffer an immediate loss of income and often remain unemployed long after their unemployment benefits are exhausted. When these workers do find new jobs, they are frequently lower-paying and have a lower occupational status than the old jobs. Often workers displaced by plant shutdowns are forced to take part-time work when they really need and want to work full-time. Secondary effects of unemployment often include mortgage foreclosures and exhaustion of savings. When economic decline and unemployment are heavily concentrated in a given locality, the unemployed worker will usually be unable to extract accumulated equity in a dwelling because of a depressed housing market. The loss of a job that confers status, gives meaning to life, connects one to the larger world, and provides an outlet for satisfaction of the social needs and the financial problems that are brought on by unemployment together result in an increased incidence of physical and mental illnesses. The social costs of unemployment go well beyond the individual directly involved. Plant shutdowns and increased unemployment levels reduce tax revenues available to all levels of government, and place increased demands on a variety of government programs, including unemployment compensation, welfare, and health care.

As Bluestone and Harrison have pointed out, these problems do not completely disappear when higher levels of economic growth return to a region as the result of the development of new industries (Bluestone & Harrison 1982, 92–98). In New England workers once employed in the older mill industries have for the most part been unable to obtain jobs in the new high-growth computer and electronics firms. These new businesses are creating relatively well-paying jobs for the highly skilled, on the one hand, and relatively low-paying jobs for the semiskilled, on the other. The result is a growth in the inequality of income distribution in the region. To summarize, regions like New England that have gone through a long period of economic retardation suffer from extraordinary unemployment levels for a lengthy span of time, and when they do experience economic recovery, many of their economic problems remain unresolved.

The central question, then, is the following: Can new economic arrangements be instituted that will short-circuit the long-wave process and prevent the suffering that results from a retardation of regional growth? The central hypothesis of the pages that follow is that cooperative ownership and control of the means of production by workers can significantly reduce economic problems associated with the regional long wave of growth and decline. In the present chapter the superiority of the worker cooperative over the conventional corporate enterprise will be addressed at a theoretical level. In Chapter 5 the empirical experience with worker cooperatives will be considered. Chapter 6 will address the issue of fostering the development of a cooperative economy.

THE STRUCTURE OF A PRODUCER COOPERATIVE

Historically, various approaches have been taken to structuring the ownership and management of a producer cooperative. Some of these approaches have met with success, while others have been characterized by failure. The structure to be presented here includes those characteristics that seem to promote economic success.[1]

Membership in a producer cooperative entitles the individual to employment at a specified rate of pay, a vote in the general assembly of all members, and a share in the cooperative's total profit. A new member is required to make a capital contribution to the cooperative that normally can be financed through a payroll deduction.[2]

The rate of pay for each job category in the cooperative is a matter to be decided by the membership. A procedure that works effectively in the Mondragon system of cooperatives in the Basque region of Spain is to link the average rate of pay to comparable industries in the local economy and then to set a maximum ratio between the highest- and lowest-paid member. Each job is then ranked according to various factors, including skill requirements and responsibility, and is assigned a number between 1 and the highest ratio permitted. A wage payment is made in accordance with that number (Thomas & Logan 1982, 131–58).

Responsibility for the management of the cooperative is normally delegated to a supervisory board elected by the general assembly from its members. The supervisory board in turn selects and oversees the activities of the cooperative's manager and management team. The general assembly can also elect other bodies, such as a workers' council to oversee personnel matters. The final authority on all major questions of policy is, however, the general assembly of all cooperative members.

Once all production costs, including wages, have been met, cooperative members share in any remaining profit or surplus. A part of the surplus can be allocated to a social account for community projects. Prudence dictates that a portion should be assigned to a reserve account to help cover unexpected contingencies and possible losses in the future. The remainder can be allocated to individual members. This allocation can take the form of a direct distribution of surplus shares to members or the distribution of surplus shares to individual capital accounts that will be retained by the cooperative until the departure of the individual member. The latter procedure should be followed in order to assure that adequate funds are available for capital investment in the cooperative. The cooperative should pay an interest rate on funds deposited in the individual capital accounts that represents the opportunity cost of capital. This is necessary to assure that capital is utilized efficiently and to provide members with a reasonable return on their individual capital accounts. To prevent sudden and massive withdrawals from the capital accounts, provisions can be made to convert capital accounts into annuities when members leave the cooperative.

THE ADVANTAGES OF COOPERATIVE OWNERSHIP FOR REGIONAL ECONOMIC DEVELOPMENT

Before presenting the advantages of cooperative ownership for regional development, the stage can best be set by reviewing the causes of regional economic decline and the role of the conventional corporate enterprise in that process. Regional economic decline, as suggested in chapters 2 and 3, is the result of the decline of aging industries and the lack of the creation of new industries to replace them. Established corporations in mature industries limit the creation of new industries because those corporations attract resources that would otherwise flow to new industries, train managers (as opposed to entrepreneurs), and provide managerial opportunities to those who would otherwise start new businesses. Only after economic decline has begun will the rate of new business formation pick up, and only after a lengthy period of new business incubation will new industries emerge. Even though mature corporations have the financial resources to start new industries and provide employment opportunities in new fields to existing employees, they seem to be structurally unable to do so. Mature corporations in aging industries are faced with the problem of producing on a relatively large scale in order to minimize production costs rather than with the problems of responding quickly to revolutionary changes in products, technologies, and markets. Their problem is managerial rather than entrepreneurial.

To solve this problem, production is organized bureaucratically, with work tasks carefully specified in job descriptions. The central responsibility of management is to monitor employees to make sure that assigned tasks are carried out. It is precisely this bureaucratic form of production organization that prevents corporations from pioneering in new lines of production. To be successful in a new industry, where products and technologies are in a state of flux and change, requires organizational flexibility rather than the organizational rigidity that characterizes bureaucratized production processes. The ability to innovate and adapt rapidly to change requires that an organization be relatively small or that it be highly decentralized, with decision-making autonomy granted to employees at relatively low levels in the organization hierarchy.[3] When mature corporations are faced with declining product markets, they simply discharge their employees in existing production facilities and redirect their capital to growing markets through acquisitions or mergers (Bluestone & Harrison 1982, 40–46). Corporations have no legal nor moral obligation to continue providing job opportunities to their employees. They are obligated to their stockholders, not their employees.

This distinction between obligation to stockholders and obligation to employees indicates the central difference between a conventional corporation and a producer cooperative. In a corporation the stockholders have the legal right to elect the board of directors, legal ownership of the net assets of the corporation, and a legal right to the profits earned by the corporation. In a producer cooperative the workers have the personal right to elect the supervisory board and to share in the surplus earnings of the cooperative. In addition, workers have property rights in the net assets of the cooperative, as reflected in their individual capital accounts. In the corporation all rights are property rights, while in the cooperative, rights are a mixture of personal rights and property rights (Ellerman 1983b). Property rights are associated with the ownership of some asset, while personal rights attach to the individual as a consequence of organizational membership. Since in a cooperative the responsibility of management and the supervisory board is to the worker-members, the result will be an incentive structure that is entirely different from that of the corporation.

As already noted, the corporation will discharge employees when it is in the stockholders' interest to do so. Being responsible to the member-owners, a cooperative will not discharge its workers, except for dereliction of work duties in individual cases and for the purpose of liquidating the enterprise in the case of bankruptcy. A producer cooperative will thus be strongly motivated to find new products in growing markets to replace older products in declining markets, and to produce the new goods with presently employed member-workers. Also, cooperatives will lack any incentive to relocate in order to take advantage of wage rate differentials or the absence of unions. In short, relative to the corporate enterprise, the producer cooperative will have a high degree of community stability.

In theory, then, the producer cooperative's response to industrial decline ought to be superior to that of the corporation, in terms of the maintenance of regional employment through the creation of new products and, therefore, of new industries. An important question remains to be answered, however: Is the structure of the producer cooperative such that it can adequately respond to economic change? The answer depends on the extent of the X-efficiency of the cooperative relative to the conventional business enterprise. The concept of X-efficiency has to do with the effectiveness of using a given set of resources. One economic organization is more X-efficient than another if it produces a larger output from a given set of resources (Leibenstein 1966). Also, one economic organization is more X-efficient than another if it is able to respond more rapidly than another to economic change. A central proposition of the analysis to follow is that the producer cooperative is more X-efficient in terms of productivity and the ability to respond to economic change than is the conventional corporate enterprise.

Since the individual worker is the central actor in transforming material inputs into outputs, analysis of X-efficiency must necessarily be founded upon a conception of human behavior in productive activity. The conventional view of human behavior in production is that individuals engage in productive activity strictly for economic reward. Individual workers enter into contractual arrangements with employers solely for the purpose of material gain. While economic reward is necessarily a fundamental motivation for engaging in productive activity, the literature on human psychology and simple intuition suggest that there are other reasons for seeking employment.[4] Individuals have certain social needs that can be satisfied in the work place. They desire to have significant social contacts with others who are similarly situated and to be an integral part of a larger social organization in which group members have a common objective. In such a situation individuals will incorporate the goals of the group as their own, not only as a result of group social pressure but also as a consequence of the moral acceptance and internalization of the group goal. The acceptance of the group goal because of social pressure essentially involves a quid pro quo; positive social acceptance is traded for individual effort toward the group goal. Internalization of the group goal comes as a result of a psychological bond with the group in which one no longer distinguishes a difference between the self and the group when it comes to effort toward meeting group ends; in this case, effort is put forth without anything tangible being received in return.

Individuals also have a desire for personal accomplishment involving the application of skills and powers to the creation of some socially useful good or the resolution of some important problems. In general, personal accomplishment requires a reasonable degree of individual or small group autonomy in the production process. A sense of personal accomplishment is unlikely to come from a job that simply involves obeying the instructions of others or carrying out some activity according to precisely defined rules. If the individual accepts the goal of the group, then identification with the group and individual autonomy need not be in conflict. The individual will seek personal accomplishment by furthering group goals. However, if the individual neither identifies with the group nor accepts its goals, then individual autonomy can result in behavior that is not in the group's interest. The individual will seek personal accomplishment by furthering individual goals.

Corporations and cooperatives both provide income in return for work. Unlike the corporation, however, the producer cooperative is linked to the individual worker in two other ways: the individual worker has a right to share in the surplus earnings of the cooperative and owns a share of the cooperative's net assets, and the individual worker has voting rights in the cooperative. The formal ties between the worker and the enterprise are thus significantly different in the corporation and the cooperative. In the corporation the worker is treated formally as an instrument of production hired by management for the purpose of expanding the net assets and earning power of the corporation (Ellerman 1983c, 22–27). In the cooperative the worker is treated as a member of an organization with clear-cut rights and responsibilities, and the obligation of the organization is to serve the welfare of its worker-members, not anonymous stockholders who in no way come under the authority of the organization.

With a clear conception of the role of human behavior in production and the fundamental differences between the corporation and the producer cooperative, the question of X-efficiency can now be addressed. X-efficiency differences can arise between the corporation and the cooperative because labor contracts are necessarily incomplete and because of differences in decision-making costs. If managers had full knowledge of the production process, and if the contribution of each worker to output could be accurately measured, then labor contracts could be fully specified and labor resources could be used to their maximum efficiency. The problem is that labor contracts cannot be fully specified because in many cases the contribution to output by individual workers cannot be accurately measured and the tasks that workers will be required to perform in order to successfully carry out production cannot always be known ahead of time (Leibenstein 1966, 407; Alchain & Demsetz 1972). Also, the more complex the labor contract, the greater the enforcement costs in terms of monitoring worker performance. Furthermore, workers themselves will gain unique or idiosyncratic knowledge of the production process that will give them bargaining power within the enterprise (Williamson 1975, ch. 4). This knowledge and bargaining power will tend to increase with the extent of autonomy the worker has over an area of production (Booth 1985). If work tasks are carefully specified through job descriptions, then workers will have little independence on the job and a limited ability to gain special knowledge of the production process. However, if individual workers are given autonomy over a major segment of the production process and the freedom to carry out production responsibilities as they see fit, then they will gain more idiosyncratic knowledge and thus will have more extensive intraorganizational bargaining power.

As a result of all these problems, the corporation is left with rather unpleasant choices in organizing its production processes. On the one hand, responsibility for segments of the production process where output is measurable could be turned over to individual workers or small groups of workers, thereby eliminating the need for a complex labor contract and resolving the problem of unforeseen work tasks arising. Workers could be remunerated in this situation according to their productivity. The problem is that they would gain idiosyncratic knowledge and the bargaining power that goes with it. On the other hand, job descriptions could be used to specify work responsibilities and the procedures to be used in meeting those responsibilities in great detail, thus reducing the potential for acquiring idiosyncratic knowledge. This of course would require an elaborate and costly managerial bureaucracy to ensure that all work tasks were carried out and to prevent the shirking of work responsibilities.[5]

Because of the threat of increased worker bargaining power, corporations generally have opted for the latter scheme of organization (Edwards 1979, ch. 8). In fact, corporations may find it rational to adopt the bureaucratic scheme of work organization even though it is technically less efficient than the decentralized autonomous mode of work organization. The problem for the corporation is its inability to assure contractually that workers will not exercise their bargaining power to extract gains beyond those generated by the autonomous form of work organization. This can occur when a substantial investment in new physical capital is required to return to the bureaucratic organization of work. Corporations would be reluctant to impose legal sanctions against workers in this situation because it is only the workers involved who would have the knowledge required to continue production (Booth 1985).

The reason that the corporation is often driven to adopt the bureaucratic mode of production organization, with its attendant labor-shirking problems and costly managerial hierarchy, can be traced in part to its property and organizational structure. As already noted, at a formal level the only obligation of the corporation to employees is to remunerate them for their labor time. The employee is simply an instrument used for the purpose of earning profits for stockholders. The appropriate psychological attitude of the employee toward the corporation is to view it simply as a source of income. Since the purpose of the corporation is to serve the interests of the stockholders rather than of the employees, and since the employees do not have any formal say in corporation decision making through legal voting rights, there is little reason to expect the employee to identify with goals of the corporation and to internalize them in any way. In fact, employees will more likely satisfy their needs for social solidarity by identifying with the needs of their fellow employees against the corporation.

This phenomenon, of course, can lead to the formation of unions to act not only as agents of employees in bargaining with corporations but also as group structures capable of satisfying members' social needs. If employees did feel a bond of loyalty to the corporate enterprise and as a result internalized its goals, then decentralized autonomous work structures could be utilized. However, because employees are unlikely to feel such bonds as a result of the structure and goals of the corporate enterprise, autonomous work structures are unlikely to be utilized because employees will use the idiosyncratic knowledge gained to pursue their own interests rather than the interest of the corporation. In other words, they will use their newfound bargaining power to extract whatever income they can from the corporation.

The structure and responsibilities of the producer cooperative mitigate the work-organization problem faced by the corporation.

The goal of the producer cooperative is to improve the well-being of its worker-members. At the most fundamental level, worker effort will be greater simply because resulting additions to profits will go to the worker-members. Some have argued that in relatively large cooperatives, individual contribution to profitability will not be enough to motivate higher effort (Alchain & Demsetz 1972). However, others have pointed out that workers in cooperatives will have a strong incentive to monitor each other's work performance (Levin 1982, 46). Unlike the corporate enterprise, where there will be social pressure from workers to limit the pace of work, in the cooperative there will be social pressure to increase work effort. Moreover, since workers own the net assets of the producer cooperative, have a right to share in its surplus, and have a right to participate in the major decisions of the enterprise through membership in the general assembly, they are more likely to identify with the cooperative as a social group and to internalize its general goals as their own. In other words, worker-members will increase their work effort because of the benefits that accrue to all worker-members as a group.

As a consequence of a psychological bond of solidarity that individuals form with their fellow worker-members, they will increase their effort toward achievement of the group goal without direct consideration of their own private rewards.[6] Given a commitment by individual workers to the goals of the group, decentralized, autonomous work arrangements become increasingly feasible. Worker-members will be less inclined to use bargaining power derived from idiosyncratic knowledge against their fellow worker-members than they would against anonymous stockholders.[7] Also, since autonomous work arrangements satisfy the individual worker's need for personal accomplishment, the implementation of such arrangements in itself is apt to increase work effort. Work effort is likely to be greater in a job that brings with it a personal sense of achievement resulting from the successful application of individual abilities than in a job that simply involves the performance of prescribed tasks.

To summarize, in terms of productive efficiency, producer cooperatives are likely to be more X-efficient than are conventional corporations. Corporations will be plagued with the problems of employee shirking, costly managerial bureaucracies, the accomplishment of work tasks not specified in labor contracts and job descriptions, and the exercise of bargaining power by employees with idiosyncratic knowledge of production. Producer cooperatives, on the other hand, will be characterized by a higher degree of employee identification with organizational objectives than will the corporation, and thus will experience greater employee effort and productive efficiency. This result recommends the producer cooperative as a preferred vehicle for accomplishing regional economic development. Higher productive efficiency would give the producer cooperative a distinct advantage in the national and world marketplaces.

Two questions remain to be addressed in analyzing the producer cooperative as the desired institutional form for short-circuiting the downside of the regional long wave. First, is decision making in the producer cooperative more or less efficient than in the corporation? Second, can the producer cooperative respond effectively to long-term changes in market conditions? The producer cooperative as outlined above involves the election of a supervisory board by workers. On the face of it, the supervisory board functions much like a board of directors in a corporation. If this is in fact the case, then there would be little difference between the efficiency of decision making in the corporation and in the producer cooperative. Decision making is delegated to the supervisory board and the management team by the worker-members. In practice, worker-members have the option of becoming more involved in decision making by requiring major decisions to be brought before the membership as a whole or a body with a somewhat broader representation of workers. This form of decision making obviously is more costly, particularly if a consensus is sought (Rothschild-Whitt 1979, 518–25; Williamson 1975, 44).

The critics of democratic decision processes usually point to the costs without recognizing the potential benefits. The interactive process involved in peer group decision making generates information and ideas not available when decision making is delegated to one person. Decisions arrived at democratically thus could be of a higher quality than delegated decisions. Producer cooperatives have the opportunity to search out the optimal middle ground between totally consensus decision making and totally delegated decision making. Because of the reluctance of corporate management to sacrifice its authority to employees, the opportunity for this kind of experimentation is indeed more limited. To summarize, there is no reason to believe that decision-making costs will be significantly greater in cooperatives than in corporations, and it may well be that in cooperatives decision making is more effective because of democratic processes. It is clearly in the interest of worker-members to avoid decision-making structures that lead to excessive costs.

As noted above, the producer cooperative, with a management that is necessarily committed to providing stable employment opportunities for its worker-members, will have a strong incentive to seek out new technologies and product lines as the old become obsolete. Will producer cooperatives in fact have the ability to do so? Part of the answer to this question has to do with the larger problem that cooperatives face in realizing scale economies in such functions as research and development, and the financing of new innovations, without sacrificing democratic principles as a result of size. This issue will be taken up in the next section, where a host of problems faced by the cooperative organizational form are considered.

Apart from this issue, the producer cooperative is characterized by a high degree of X-efficiency in innovation for the same reasons it can achieve a high level of X-efficiency in the use of productive resources. Since worker-members as a group will benefit from innovations that increase surplus or provide stable employment opportunities, they will individually have a strong incentive to seek out changes that benefit the group, given the psychic identification of individual and group. In addition, the ability to organize production in decentralized autonomous groupings makes it possible for individuals and small groups to utilize their skills to come up with new innovations. This is much less the case in bureaucratically organized enterprises, where work tasks are carefully specified. Innovation requires a degree of autonomy.

Finally, little internal opposition to change is to be expected in producer cooperatives, since change will be to the benefit of the group. Individual worker-members need not be concerned about continued employment with the enterprise after a major change has taken place, since memberhsip in the cooperative assures employment. This is not the case with the conventional corporation. Also, the cooperative will have a stronger incentive than the corporation to invest in retraining worker-members, since they are likely to be with the cooperative for a long period of time because of the stable employment opportunities and because they are unlikely to use special knowledge gained as a basis for bargaining for higher wages.

THE LIMITATIONS OF THE PRODUCER COOPERATIVE

In theory, producer cooperatives are more X-efficient than conventional corporations. If this is the case in practice, why are there so few producer cooperatives in existence? What are the basic limitations of cooperatives, and how can those limitations be overcome?

The key problems facing producer cooperatives include inadequate capital investment, a limited incentive for growth, difficulties in balancing effective democratic control with the attainment of scale economies, and problems in the initial organization. These problems taken together explain why producer cooperatives are unlikely to emerge on their own in great numbers. However, these problems can be overcome through institutional reforms. The task of this section is, first, to explain the problems faced by cooperative in the framework of a market-capitalist economy, and then to indicate how modifications to cooperative organizational structures and the creation of support institutions can remove the barriers to the formation of producer cooperatives.

One of the central problems facing cooperatives is the financing of capital investment. In raising equity capital, cooperatives must rely entirely on their members. To permit outside investment would violate cooperative principles. Being fearful of their unconventional structure, financial institutions have been reluctant to provide debt capital to cooperative enterprises. As a result, cooperative enterprises have often started out being woefully undercapitalized. Worker-members seldom have sufficient access to capital on their own to properly capitalize a new business venture.

Cooperatives that are successful in getting started often face ongoing problems in achieving and maintaining an adequate level of investment because of limited incentives for worker-members to reinvest surplus earnings. This problem is of greatest significance in those cooperatives where the price of membership shares is not market-determined or where there are no disembodied individual capital accounts paying interest on surplus earnings assigned to individual members. If worker-members simply pay a predetermined membership fee and if capital investment is financed from retained earnings, then a worker who remains with the cooperative for a period of time that is less than the life of the investment will not receive a full return on the investment through the resulting surplus earnings.[8] The worker-investor is not paid a direct return for invested surplus earnings, but receives the return indirectly through higher future surplus earnings. Consequently, if a worker-member leaves the cooperative prior to the time the return from the investment project is fully realized, then that worker-member will not receive the full benefit of the project. The result will be a division of interest between members who plan to stay with the cooperative for a long period of time and those who plan to stay a relatively short period of time. Democratic decision making on investment projects would thus lead to a lower level of investment in the cooperative than is economically desirable. If there is a strong sense of solidarity among workers and a resulting desire by all workers to see the cooperative continue in the long run, then the importance of this problem would be reduced.

Some cooperatives have a requirement that whatever level of capital investment is undertaken be maintained in perpetuity or until the cooperative is dissolved, when the value of any remaining assets is given to a charitable institution or some other third party. This requirement also discourages investment by worker-members. In this situation, worker-members will capture the return on investment from higher surplus earnings if they remain with the cooperative for the life of the investment, but they will never be able to get back the amount of the investment. Consequently, the only projects to be accepted will be those that have a return sufficiently above the rate of interest that can be earned elsewhere to compensate for the loss of the original cost of the investment.

Both of these problems can be resolved by establishing a market for worker-member shares. Entering worker-members would pay a market value for the right to membership that would fully capture the future earnings potential of the cooperative. Departing worker-members thus would fully capture the future value of internally financed investments. The difficulty with this approach is that entering worker-members could be required to raise a substantial amount of capital in order to obtain membership. The cooperative could ease the problem of new member entry by establishing a loan fund and a payroll deduction scheme to pay for the new member's share. Still, entering members could well be burdened with a large payroll deduction for a considerable period of time if the present value of future surplus earnings is substantial.

An alternative to marketable shares that reduces the burden on entering workers is the establishment of disembodied individual capital accounts. As already noted, under such an arrangement undistributed surplus earnings would be assigned to individuals and a market rate of interest would be paid on such earnings until they are withdrawn at the time of the worker-member's departure from the cooperative. All members would thus be paid a market rate of return on their investment and would receive the full amount of the investment back.

While this arrangement substantially improves the incentive for undertaking investments in the cooperative, a problem still remains. Investment projects will affect the flow of future surplus earnings, and different projects will likely have different surplus earnings time patterns. As a result, disagreement can still arise between long-term and short-term members over which investment project to undertake if one yields high returns in the early years and another yields high returns in later years. One can easily imagine such a situation arising when a cooperative is confronted with a need to invest heavily in new product development because of declining markets for existing products. Worker-members nearing retirement would likely prefer short-term investments that would improve near-term competitiveness in existing product markets, while younger workers would desire the cooperative to undertake long-term investments in new product markets. The ability of the cooperative to respond to changing market conditions would thus be impaired. The importance of this problem would depend on the degree of solidarity among workers within the cooperative and the extent to which individual cooperative members consider the interests of fellow members.

A final problem associated with capital investment in a cooperative should be noted. In contrast with the capitalist enterprise, the worker-members of a cooperative bear the risk associated not only with employment but also with capital investment. As already suggested, employment risk is reduced in the cooperative relative to the corporation because of the cooperative's responsibility to provide its worker-members with employment opportunities. On the other side of the equation, however, the worker bears capital investment risk. The bearing of this risk provides an added incentive to worker-members to make sure that the enterprise is managed and operated efficiently, and that the cooperative is always looking to the future to anticipate market changes.

While individual producer cooperatives have a commitment to provide employment opportunities for their existing membership, they have limited incentives to provide growth in employment opportunities and to respond to changes in product demand (Ward 1958). This conclusion is based on the assumption that producer cooperatives will operate in such a way as to maximize the average income of their member-workers. If this is the case, then a new worker-member will be added to the cooperative only if doing so increases revenues net of nonlabor costs by an amount that is at least equal to the current average income of workers. To do otherwise would reduce the existing income per worker. A conventional business, on the other hand, will increase employment so long as the addition to net revenues is at least equal to the wage rate paid to the newly hired workers. If this wage rate for a conventional business is less than the average income for members of a producer cooperative with an identical technology and productivity, then the conventional business will employ more workers than the cooperative.[9]

Also, it is possible, in theory, that the producer cooperative will respond in a perverse manner to an increase in product demand and price. A higher price would increase both the average income per worker and the addition to net revenue of the last worker admitted to membership in the cooperative. Theoretical economists have shown that the average income per worker would rise by a greater amount than the addition to net revenue of the last worker hired. The cooperative would thus have an incentive to reduce the size of its membership and possibly to decrease output.[10] If membership brings with it a guarantee of continued employment and a right to remain a member, then obviously a reduction in membership can come about only through attrition. A reduction in membership will thus be unlikely to occur immediately. By comparison, the conventional firm will respond to a price increase with an increase of output because the addition to net revenue from hiring an added worker is increased while the wage rate is likely to remain constant or to rise by an amount less than the increase of net revenue. Hence, the conventional enterprise will respond positively to an increase in product demand while the producer cooperative will respond negatively or not at all.[11]

Finally, it should be noted that competition will, in theory, drive the average income in a producer cooperative down to the prevailing wage rate in the long run, causing the output level of the producer cooperative and conventional firm in the same field with the same cost schedules to converge. In the long run, then, there is no difference between resource allocation in a conventional enterprise and a producer cooperative. The only difference arises in the short run.[12] As argued above, there is, however, a distinct difference between the two in terms of X-efficiency.

The perverse supply response analysis assumes that worker-members in a cooperative adjust employment, and not hours, to meet changing demand conditions. In practice, the adjustment of hours can be a partial antidote to the perverse supply problem. As product demand and price increase, worker-members will increase their hours if the resulting added income outweighs the implicit value of forgone leisure time (M. D. Berman, 1977). Of course, the ability to expand output of a given labor force by increasing hours is inherently limited.

The central problem with the perverse supply analysis is the basic assumption of average income maximization. Little is known about the actual objectives that producer cooperatives set for themselves (Ellerman 1983b, 26). In contrast with the capitalist corporation, objectives are arrived at through a democratic process, and as a result may well differ from one cooperative to another. It is conceivable that cooperative members may feel a responsibility for creating employment opportunities, and thus may be willing to forgo some income in order to expand. Also, cooperative members may see that long-term survival depends on meeting growth of consumer demand. The failure to supply key customers in a period of peak demand could lead to their permanent loss. A cooperative may thus decide to forgo higher current surplus and add worker-members in order to be able to meet customer demands.

Also, if producer cooperatives have market power, strategic considerations could enter into output and hiring decisions. Like an oligopolist corporation choosing a target profit level that discourages entry of new enterprises, a producer cooperative may place an upper limit on average member income. If it does so, then as demand increases, it can add members while maintaining its target average member income as long as the net revenue added by the marginal member is greater than the target average income. In fact, one could imagine a producer cooperative selecting a target average income even when faced with extensive market competition and then pursuing other group-determined goals subject to that constraint. The neoclassical theory of the producer cooperative is distinctly limited because it cannot possibly take account of the multiplicity of goals that could arise from a group decision-making process. What these goals would be can be established only by a careful study of cooperative behavior in the real world.

One final point needs to be made with respect to the question of employment growth and cooperatives. The capitalist corporation will invest in new enterprises and production facilities when an appropriate rate of return can be earned. A producer cooperative will do so under the average-income-maximizing assumption only if the net result is an increase in average worker-member income. Thus the capitalist corporation will invest in some cases where the producer cooperative will not (Schweikart 1982, 72). For example, if a second plant yielded the same per-worker income as an existing plant, a producer cooperative operating the first plant would have no particular incentive to invest in the second. If the rate of return were adequate in both plants, the corporation would have an incentive to invest its capital in the second plant. The producer cooperative is thus biased against employment expansion, as it is biased against employment contraction. The question of devising institutional arrangements to overcome the bias against growth will be considered in the next section.

Before considering measures to resolve the difficulties faced by cooperatives, two other problems need to be considered: the question of balancing scale economies against democratic decision making, and the problem faced by cooperatives in their initial organization. To achieve scale economies in certain lines of production may require a relatively large cooperative. Democratic decision making is less effective in large groups than it is in small ones (Thomas & Logan 1982, 35). If this is the case, then scale economies will have to be sacrificed for effective democratic decision making or vice versa. Since there are many sectors of the economy where average production facility size is not very large, this does not preclude the building of a large cooperative sector (Stein 1974, 1–25).

The final problem facing cooperatives—though perhaps the most significant of all, it has received surprisingly little attention in the literature—is the distinct lack of economic incentives in the context of market capitalism for the formation of producer cooperatives. For the conventional capitalist enterprise, there is a substantial incentive for an individual or small group to undertake the task of organizing a business venture. The stockholders, by virtue of property ownership, are assured title to the future profits of a successful enterprise, and the organizing agents can assure themselves a significant share in these profits by assigning themselves a major portion of the stock. This is not the case with a producer cooperative. The organizing agents of a producer cooperative will have a right to share in future surplus earnings on an equal basis with other, similarly situated worker-members. An organizing agent ultimately could become a manager, and as a consequence receive a somewhat higher salary and share of the surplus than the typical member, but in the case of a cooperative the present value of future earnings for such an agent is likely to be much less than that in a conventional capitalist enterprise. The capitalist entrepreneur can appropriate all or a significant share of future profits, depending on the degree of equity participation by others in the venture, while the cooperative entrepreneur is likely to receive a relatively small share of future surplus earnings.

As a result of the difference in property and personal rights arrangements in a capitalist firm and a cooperative, the organization of the enterprise is a private goods problem in the case of the capitalist firm and a collective goods problem in the case of the producer cooperative. The membership of a cooperative will benefit as a group from its initial organization, but there is no assurance that the benefit to any single member or small group of members will be adequate to offset the cost of initial organization, unless the organizing agent receives some sort of nonpecuniary benefit from the act of carrying out initial organization. In addition, there is a potential for worker-members to act as free riders by holding back their contributions to the costs of initial organization in the expectation that others will bear the burden. The final result will be that insufficient resources will be devoted to the initial organization of the cooperative, thereby leading to its failure.

To summarize, producer cooperatives not only face difficulties raising adequate capital, generating economic growth, and achieving economies of scale, but also must contend with a significant lack of incentives for anyone to bring them into existence.

OVERCOMING THE LIMITATIONS OF
OF PRODUCER COOPERATIVES

The key to overcoming the problems faced by producer cooperatives is the creation of a financial institution to which individual cooperatives can be tied contractually. This institution will be referred to as a cooperative bank. The first step in the analysis that follows is to describe the structure of the cooperative bank, and the second step is to consider how a cooperative bank can resolve the basic problems faced by cooperatives.[13]

The basic function of the cooperative bank would be to accept deposits from, and to make short- and long-term loans to, associated producer cooperatives. To augment its capital, a cooperative bank could accept deposits or investments from the public or from local, state, and federal government agencies. To assure an adequate and growing supply of capital, the cooperative bank could require associated producer cooperatives to retain all or some part of surplus earnings in individual worker-member capital accounts that would be deposited with the bank. This amounts to requiring worker-members in producer cooperatives to save a portion of their income, but it is a necessary measure in order to assure an adequate level of capital accumulation. The disembodied individual capital accounts discussed above should thus be structurally linked to the cooperative bank.

The bank itself could be restricted to making loans to associated enterprises so as to ensure that its capital flows to producer cooperatives. In order to have an adequate outlet for bank loans, the bank should have a venture development division whose function would be to assist in the creation of new producer cooperatives. This division would maintain a catalog of up-to-date marketing studies on feasible products for new enterprises, assist those wanting to organize cooperatives with the development of business plans, and provide seed money to the individuals who actually undertake the task of organizing the cooperatives (Ellerman 1984). The bank also could reduce the needs of cooperatives for managerial staff by providing management services in such areas as finance and accounting to the individual producer cooperatives. Control of the bank would be vested in a supervisory board composed not only of bank employees but also of representatives of associated cooperatives. To provide bank worker-members with an incentive to serve the needs of the associated cooperatives, distributions of surplus to their capital accounts could be tied to the average per-member surplus earnings in the associated producer cooperatives. This would also provide for a degree of equality in earnings between bank and producer cooperative worker-members.

How would the cooperative bank resolve the problems of capitalization, growth, attaining adequate scale, and initial organization that face the individual producer cooperatives?

Given that the cooperative bank is adequately capitalized, then the problem producer cooperatives face in obtaining initial capital is for all practical purposes solved. Individual cooperatives need not rely entirely on their membership for capital funds. Needed capital can now be borrowed from the cooperative bank. Worker-members will still be required to invest in the cooperative initially, but additional capital will be available through the bank. In addition, bank funds can be used to make loans to workers for their initial capital requirement, thus eliminating the need for worker-members to put up cash in order to gain membership.

The problem of ongoing capital needs is also solved. Whenever a cooperative wishes to undertake added investment, it can borrow the funds from the bank at a market rate of interest. So long as the cooperatives as a group generate a surplus, the bank will be assured of a growing source of loanable funds as a result of the requirement that some portion of the surplus be allocated to individual capital accounts that are deposited in the bank. The bank will pay a competitive rate of interest on deposits in the individual capital accounts. Worker-members will thus receive a market-determined rate of return on their capital account savings. Producer cooperatives will have an incentive to invest in capital projects so long as the returns on the projects are at least sufficient to pay the opportunity cost of capital to the bank. Disincentives for investment common to producer cooperatives are essentially eliminated through these institutional measures.

In order for the individual capital accounts to become a source of finance, through the bank, to the system of associated cooperatives, a well-defined wage determination process would be needed. Otherwise, individual producer cooperatives could vote wage increases that would eliminate surplus earnings, and therefore deposits in capital accounts. One approach would be to link the average wage rate in the producer cooperative to the average wage rate in comparable enterprises in the local economy. The actual wage paid to any particular individual in the cooperative would depend on that person's skills and responsibilities. To ensure a reasonable level of worker-member solidarity, an upper limit on income inequality could be set by requiring that the highest-paid member receive no more than a specified multiple of the lowest-paid worker's income. This limit would also have to reflect the pay level required to attract highly skilled members. If greater solidarity is desired between cooperatives, the same benchmark wage could be used for all cooperatives.

As already noted, disembodied capital accounts have one disadvantage; they do not fully resolve the problem of different time horizons in investment decisions for different worker-members. For example, if there are two competing investment projects that provide a return over and above the opportunity cost of capital, and one project augments surplus earnings in the near future while the other does so in the distant future, there could be disagreement between worker-members who are close to retirement and those who have a long time to go before retirement. How significant this problem would be in practice is hard to say, although in the previous section a plausible example was presented where older workers would be resistant to investment in new product development.

The problem could be resolved by combining disembodied capital accounts with marketable memberships. The capital accounts would accumulate the value of all past retained earnings. The marketable memberships would reflect the expected value of future surplus earnings over and above the opportunity costs of capital. Departing worker-members would thus benefit from future income streams arising from current capital investment decisions, and would therefore take a long-term perspective in capital investment decision making. Another alternative would be to have marketable memberships without individual capital accounts. The problem with this approach is that the membership price would reflect not only future surplus earnings but also the value of the capital stock financed out of past retained earnings. This could cause the price of membership to be substantial, and thus could require a very large payroll deduction to pay for the membership. Since the capital account includes the value of past savings and investment, a marketable membership combined with a capital account would carry with it a lower market price than a marketable membership alone.

To summarize, a cooperative bank combined with disembodied individual capital accounts and marketable memberships would resolve all the basic investment problems faced by cooperatives. The only remaining objection to cooperatives is that they do not permit workers to spread their capital investment risk. This could be partially resolved if associated cooperatives pooled a part of their surplus earnings for distribution to individual capital accounts. The cost of doing so would be a moderate diminution of incentives for increasing productivity, since a productivity improvement would increase not only the surplus earnings of the individual cooperative but also the pooled surplus earnings, thereby reducing the gain to the individual cooperative.

As suggested in the previous section, individual cooperatives have a limited incentive for employment growth. If a group of producer cooperatives associates with a cooperative bank, the limitation on an individual cooperative's growth are offset by the strong incentive for growth of the cooperative system as a whole. This incentive for growth is based on the accumulation of retained surplus earnings in the individual capital accounts that are deposited in the cooperative bank. Since the cooperative bank is limited to making loans to associated producer cooperatives, in order to have a market for its loans, it will have to be constantly fostering the creation of new producer cooperatives. To illustrate this point, suppose that all existing associated cooperatives have achieved a stable level of total capital investment and are earning a stable level of surplus earnings each year, with some portion of these earnings being deposited with the cooperative bank. The existing cooperatives will have no demand for additional loans from the bank, on the one hand, but will be adding to the bank's deposits, on the other. The only way the bank can loan those funds out will be through the creation of new cooperatives that will require new loans. Thus the cooperative bank is institutionally required to foster the development of new cooperatives and to create new employment opportunities. The problem of limited cooperative growth is solved.

The problem of individual cooperatives achieving scale economies without sacrificing effective democratic decision making is also solved through the organizing of individual cooperatives as a part of a larger system. Basically, scale economies can be achieved in the system as a whole without increasing the size of the individual cooperatives or significantly sacrificing their individual autonomy. The cooperative bank, for example, can achieve scale economies in the accounting and financial consulting services it provides the individual cooperatives. Groups of cooperatives can create separate entities of appropriate scale to serve their needs in such areas as marketing and research and development. If any single cooperative becomes too large for effective democratic decision making, a separable segment of its production process can be spun off as a separate cooperative.

The central problem of initial organization of producer cooperatives is clearly diminished through the institutionalizing of the entrepreneurial function in the cooperative bank (Ellerman 1984). Because the bank needs expanding producer cooperative lending opportunities, it will have a strong incentive to assist individuals and groups in the formation of new cooperative enterprises. By providing comprehensive assistance to those who wish to start a cooperative enterprise, the bank substantially reduces the risks and costs associated with a new business enterprise. This reduction of risk and cost diminishes the collective goods problem associated with starting a new cooperative venture. The individual or small group that undertakes the initial organization of the cooperative can be paid for the efforts through a bank loan that will become a part of the initial capitalization of the enterprise. The assistance and capital provided by the bank would likely attract individuals who are capable of organizing new business ventures but would not otherwise do so on their own because of the difficulty they would normally face in getting capital and the high risk of failure.

SHORT-CIRCUITING THE REGIONAL LONG WAVE

The central thesis of this book is that a system of cooperatives like the one just described is more capable of short-circuiting the long wave than the conventional corporate enterprise. As outlined in chapters 2 and 3, retardation of regional growth occurs because of the economic decline of aging industries and the lack of the new business formation necessary for the creation of new, high-growth industries to replace the old. New business formation is inadequate while the region is still experiencing growth on the basis of older industries because those industries absorb individuals who otherwise would start new businesses as well as capital and local inputs that would otherwise be available to new enterprises. Hence, at the point where the older industries begin to experience employment decline, new industries have not yet been developed as a consequence of new business formation. New business formation increases only after decline has set in, and a lengthy period of new business incubation must pass before new high-growth industries emerge. Corporations in aging industries react to decline by withdrawing capital from existing businesses in the region and redirecting that capital, through acquisitions and mergers, to new industries located in other regions.[14] Because the responsibility of the cooperative is to its existing employees, this sort of behavior is precluded. When the decline of existing product market demand is foreseen, it is the responsibility of the cooperative to seek out new product markets in order to maintain employment opportunities for its existing membership.

The ability of cooperatives to shift to new product markets is significantly increased by the presence of the cooperative bank. The venture development section of the bank, with a staff having expertise in searching out new product markets, would be of great assistance to a cooperative that needs to move into a new product line in order to survive. In addition, a source of capital would be readily available in the bank for investment in a new product line. The bank, by virtue of its organizational and financial structure, is required to be constantly creating new business ventures, even when a region is experiencing growth on the basis of existing enterprises. Consequently, new business formation and the development of new industries is likely to be taking place even before the growth retardation stage of the long wave sets in. In essence, the responsibility of the cooperative bank, together with its associated producer cooperatives, is to maintain existing, and to create new, employment opportunities in a given geographic region. The conventional corporate enterprise, by virtue of its property structure, is concerned not with the employees and their economic well-being but with the economic welfare of its stockholders.

HUMAN NEEDS IN WORK AND PRODUCER COOPERATIVES

If the only need individuals seek to satisfy through work is material sustenance, then there would be little to recommend the producer cooperative over the corporation, apart from any material advantages. The individual would view his or her treatment as an instrument of production by a business enterprise with indifference. The structure of property and personal rights in the enterprise would be of little consequence so long as a given material reward was forthcoming.

In fact, individuals engage in work for reasons that go beyond the need for material sustenance. Work can be a means by which the need to exercise skills in the creation of something of personal or social significance is satisfied, and through cooperative work the means are provided for a significant connection to a social group. As argued above, the corporate form of property formally treats the individual employee as an instrument for the advancement of the welfare of the corporate shareholders, and it is the shareholders rather than the employees who have legal voting rights in the corporation. Since the corporate organization bears no responsibility to the employee apart from those spelled out in the wage contract, and since the employee has no right to determine the nature of the corporation as an organization and as a social group, it is difficult to imagine that the corporation could be an object of significant social connection, other than the perverse one of the corporate employees organizing as a social group against the interests of the corporation and for the interests of the employees. Since the employees are unlikely to identify with the corporation and its objectives, the corporation will be reluctant to give them the autonomy they require to fulfill their needs for personal accomplishment. Rather, jobs will be structured, insofar as possible, according to carefully specified rules and bureaucratic procedures.

In the case of the producer cooperative with both property and voting rights invested in the worker-members, the situation is clearly different. Through self-government the worker-members have the right to shape the organization of the enterprise, and through ownership they have the right to the full net results of their productive efforts. Consequently, there are solid grounds for a strong social bond between the individual worker-member and the group, and individuals can be given a degree of autonomy in their work so as to satisfy the need for personal accomplishment.

Judging by the recent attempts of the modern corporation to develop an internal culture, the question of employees internalizing organizational values is not a trivial one. Corporations attempt to develop a system of values, myths, heroes, and symbols that are reinforced through rituals and ceremonies to win the allegiance of middle management employees (Dugger 1985, 8). The ultimate goal of such practices is to gain control over middle managers through an internalization of corporate goals. There is nothing wrong with individuals identifying with group values. Since such identifications do occur, they constitute an important human need. The problem in the corporation is that the values involved in the corporate culture are determined from the top down. In the cooperative the opportunity exists for the determination of group culture from the bottom up. In any organization there is always a danger that the individual will be submerged in the group values and will lose his or her identity and freedom. Since there is no forum for the expression of the values of autonomy and freedom in the authoritarian corporation, and that forum exists in the cooperative, the potential for loss of freedom would be less in the latter. Also, a group culture developed from the bottom up would in all probability command greater acceptance and emotional allegiance than one imposed from the top down.

NOTES

1. The model presented here is based on the institutional framework of the Mondragon system of cooperatives located in the Basque region of Spain. This model is described in Ellerman 1983a; and Thomas & Logan 1982.

2. Historically, capital contributions have taken two forms in cooperatives. The capital contribution can be made through the purchase of a marketable share or by the payment of a fixed membership fee. The former approach is used in plywood cooperatives located in the Pacific Northwest, while the latter is used in the Mondragon cooperative (K. V. Berman 1967; Ellerman 1983a). In the Mondragon cooperatives, the membership fee is deposited in a capital account for the individual worker-member. The capital account is discussed in more detail below, as are the relative advantages of the two forms of capital contribution.

3. See Chapter 2, section "Barriers to Corporate Innovation."

4. For a more extensive treatment of this issue, see Booth 1985. The hypothesis that individuals seek more than just material rewards from work is suggested by Maslow's hierarchy of needs (Maslow 1954, 90). Maslow argues that higher-order needs include belongingness and love, esteem, and self-actualization. Survey studies confirm that work satisfies important nonmaterial needs (*Work in America* 1973, 1–28; Sheppard & Herrick 1972).

5. The argument presented here is somewhat different from that suggested by Williamson (1975, ch. 4). He suggests that in bureaucratic enterprises the problem of individual worker monopoly over production knowledge is avoided by attaching wages to jobs rather than to individual workers. If workers were still sufficiently autonomous to gain unique ("idiosyncratic," in Williamson's terminology) knowledge of the production process that they could refuse to pass on, they would have bargaining power within the organization. Even though individuals or small groups are institutionally prohibited from bargaining over wages, they could use their power to bargain over other issues, such as promotions, working conditions, or days off. What bureaucratic control attempts to do is to define precisely each and every task in a job to the greatest extent possible, and thus permit management to retain full knowledge of the production process. Without worker identification with the goals of the enterprise, managers will structure jobs so as to avoid worker autonomy and the ability of employees to gain unique knowledge and skills that would endow them with increased bargaining strength. Williamson recognizes the nature of the problem in controlling labor, but he incorrectly specifies the nature of the solution.

6. Consider a simple example. Suppose a worker observes that a piece of machinery on an assembly line is about to break down. In the corporate setting he has little reason to report the problem. In fact, he may gain some free time because of the breakdown. In the producer cooperative a worker

with some moral commitment to the well-being of his or her fellow workers will likely report the problem because there would be a loss of production and income to the group as a whole. In the corporate setting, the worker has no reason at all to worry about the income of the stockholders.

7.   Apart from considerations of worker solidarity, individuals or small groups of individuals may refrain from exercising their bargaining power because they recognize that if they don't, other groups within the cooperative will also exercise their bargaining power, to the detriment of the cooperative as a whole. The net result of all groups or individuals exercising their bargaining power could be a rise in average production costs that would harm the cooperative's competitive position in the market. This problem is that of an n-person game with a cooperative solution that has greater total benefits than the solution where each pursues his or her private interest. Over the long run the group may well recognize that it would be better off accepting the cooperative solution of not exploiting bargaining power, particularly if the group is relatively small. In a corporation, workers can exploit stockholders by exercising their bargaining power. This is not the case in the cooperative, where all surplus earnings accrue to the workers.

8.   For a more extensive theoretical analysis of this problem, see Stephen 1982, 10–14. This problem was first discussed in detail by Vanek (1977, 171–98). Also see Furabotn 1976; Berman & Berman 1978.

9.   This conclusion assumes equal X-efficiency, an assumption that is likely to be incorrect.

10.   In theory, output could either increase or decrease, depending on the amount of capital added. The average income-maximizing level of employment will always decline, however.

11.   Again, if capital investment is altered, this conclusion could be changed. If employment is held steady in the cooperative and capital is added, then output would increase.

12.   If production technology is characterized by fixed coefficients in the use of inputs, there will be no difference between the producer cooperative and the conventional firm in either the short run or the long run.

13.   The description of the cooperative bank is based on the structure of the bank in the Mondragon system of cooperatives (Thomas & Logan 1982). Modifications of this basic structure to suit the situation in the United States will be taken up in Chapter 6.

14.   The strategy behind this is nicely described in Dugger 1985.

5

THE COOPERATIVE ALTERNATIVE: PRACTICE

In theory, producer cooperatives would appear to have distinct advantages over conventional corporate enterprises. They have a greater potential for evening out the swings in regional long waves, providing secure employment opportunities, producing efficiently, and serving the needs for social identification and personal accomplishment in work. These conclusions are thus far only based on theoretical arguments. What is the situation in practice? The problem with investigating the performance and behavior of producer cooperatives in practice is that there are not very many of them. This is not surprising, in light of the theoretical prediction that cooperatives in a market capitalist world will be faced with a collective goods problem in initial organization and difficulties in raising adequate capital. Nonetheless, producer cooperatives in various forms have existed, and do exist, in Western industrial economies, and some tentative conclusions can be reached about their performance and behavior.

The purpose of this chapter is to summarize some of the findings on producer cooperative performance and behavior. In Chapter 4 the claim was made that producer cooperatives will produce more efficiently than their conventional counterparts. Is this in fact the case, and if so, why? The claim was also made that cooperatives will respond effectively to long-term changes in product demand. Is there any evidence to support this contention? Have cooperatives in fact faced a significant problem in attracting investment capital? If so, how have they overcome the problem? Are cooperatives in practice faced with limited prospects for economic growth? How do cooperatives resolve the competing demands for achieving scale economies and maintaining effective democratic decision making? How, historically, have cooperatives overcome the barriers to initial organization?

COOPERATIVE MOVEMENT HISTORY

Before addressing these questions in detail, it is useful to summarize certain elements of the history of the cooperative movement. The cooperative movement has its historical roots and most significant development in commercial endeavors rather than in production. The real beginning of the cooperative movement occurred with the establishment of a retail trading cooperative in England by the Rochdale Pioneers in 1844.[1]

The flannel weavers of Rochdale and other workers who participated in the early cooperative movement were responding to two forces. On the one hand there was the capitalist employer who was always seeking to reduce their wages, while on the other there was the local shopkeeper who was always desiring to raise the prices of the necessities of life he sold them (Kress 1941, 8). To extract themselves from this set of circumstances, the Rochdale cooperators wanted not only to establish their own retailing facility but also to start their own manufacturing ventures so as to provide themselves with employment.

The ultimate conception of the cooperative movement, at least in one view, was a society organized by a democracy of consumers and based on production for use rather than for profit (Webb & Webb 1921, 185–86). The central principles established in the Rochdale retail cooperative included the selling of goods at prevailing prices, a fixed rate of interest paid on capital, the distribution of profits to members in proportion to purchases, no credit, one vote per member regardless of capital holdings, and regular meetings for the discussion of the cooperative's business (Kress 1941, 24). In these rules primacy of control is given to the consumer rather than to the workers in the cooperative. Nonetheless, many in the early cooperative movement subscribed to democratic control by workers and the distribution of profits to workers. However, this view did not prevail in the movement in England; and the retailing and wholesaling cooperatives, and any associated production facilities, maintained the principle of consumer control (Webb & Webb 1921, 228; Kress 1941, 38).

While retailing and wholesaling cooperatives nowhere dominate retail or wholesale activity in its entirety, in a number of European countries they have gained a significant share of the market (Gottlieb 1984, 137). Those who have analyzed the cooperative movement attribute its success to the dividend on sales, arguing that it encourages membership in and continuous trade with the coop. In fact, the cooperative movement's success can most likely be attributed to its ability to attain efficiencies associated with relatively large-scale facilities. Because of low initial capital requirements and the attraction of self-employment, retail trade has a tendency toward proliferation of undersized, inefficient operations. So long as profits are above normal in a given area, new retailers will enter the market and, in the process, reduce the amount of trade per retailer until profits reach a relatively low level (Gottlieb 1984, 134–35). This practice opened up an opportunity for cooperatives that could attract large memberships and thus operate on a more efficient scale.[2] In contrast with the European experience, retail and wholesale cooperatives in urban areas have been relatively less successful in the United States. While a number of reasons have been suggested for this, including the heterogeneity of the population, individualist values and the lack of interest in cooperative ideals, and the mobility of the U.S. population, one of the most probable reasons for a lack of cooperative success is the early growth of large chain stores and mail order houses in the United States that took advantage of scale economies in retailing (Kress 1941, 66–67; Gottlieb 1984, 135).

The cooperative movement also has been relatively successful in agriculture in both the United States and Europe (Gottlieb 1984, 141). The farmer, like the urban wage earner, is caught in between conflicting economic forces. The manufacturers and the middlemen, who provide the inputs the farmer needs, desire to keep the prices paid by the farmer as high as possible, while those who purchase the output of the farmer want to keep the prices they pay to the farmer as low as possible.[3] By forming purchasing cooperatives the farmers can bargain more effectively with manufacturers for farm implements, fertilizers, insecticides, pesticides, and seeds. By instituting marketing cooperatives farmers can store their crops until the best possible price can be obtained and can deliver them in large volumes. Cooperatives have also played a major role in improving the efficiency of marketing for agricultural products; and cooperative financing institutions, often established with the assistance of government, play a major role in meeting the substantial credit needs of farmers.

In contrast with retailing and farm cooperatives, producer cooperatives founded on the principles of democratic self-management and the distribution of surplus earnings to employees have not histor-

ically experienced anywhere near the same degree of economic success. Historians of the cooperative movement have often written off
producer cooperatives as impractical. The Webbs argue, for example, that the principle of self-management is fundamentally flawed
because the manager who is in the position of giving orders in the
normal course of the day to a staff of workers must then turn around
and satisfy the wishes of the workers or be dismissed. They also argue
that workers will resist the introduction of innovations and new kinds
of labor, and that there will be a tendency for successful producer cooperatives to employ labor hired for wages and, as a result, revert to
being a capitalist enterprise (Webb & Webb 1921, 464–65). Indeed,
there were many failures of producer cooperatives in the 19th century,
including the Rochdale Cooperative Manufacturing Society, which
was to produce cotton cloth under worker self-government and profit
sharing. Since the stock was predominantly in the hands of outsiders,
the stockholders eliminated profit sharing with the workers and the
enterprise became little different from an ordinary joint-stock company (Kress 1941, 26).

The picture painted by historians of the early producer cooperative movement thus was not very bright. They saw the movement fail-
ing because of internal management problems, lack of access to capital, a failure to innovate to meet changing market conditions, and a
tendency to convert successful producer cooperatives to capitalist
ownership. The retailing cooperatives, on the other hand, were successful because they needed less capital and could raise capital in
small amounts from a relatively large membership. Unlike manufacturing enterprises, the retailing cooperatives could be started on a
shoestring and expanded as membership grew. The farm cooperatives were relatively successful because of the farmers' universal dis-
like of the middleman, community solidarity, acquired experience in
business affairs, dependency on local suppliers and marketing
agents, and considerable need for credit (Gottlieb 1984, 139–40).

While the early producer cooperative experience is not very encouraging, a more recent experience has been documented suggesting
that producer cooperatives deserve further evaluation as a valid
means for organizing productive efforts. Despite the assessment of
the Webbs, a producer cooperative sector in England has continued
to exist from the peak of the movement in 1893 until the present, although the number of societies has been shrinking. In contrast with
the English experience, the French producer cooperative sector has

been experiencing significant expansion in recent years, as have the Italian producer cooperatives. Even in U.S. history one can find examples of producer cooperatives that endured for relatively lengthy periods of time and experienced economic success. Finally, since 1956 a very successful system of cooperatives associated with a cooperative bank has emerged in the Basque region of Spain. Although the cooperative historical experience is limited in comparison with other, more conventional modes of production organization, it appears to be extensive enough to draw at least some preliminary conclusions regarding the potential for the development of a substantial cooperative economic sector. Consequently, in the remainder of this chapter the producer cooperative experience will be used to evaluate the theoretical issues set forth above on producer cooperative efficiency, ability to respond to economic change, capital investment, growth, ability to achieve scale economies, and initial organization.

THE QUESTION OF ECONOMIC EFFICIENCY

In Chapter 4 it was hypothesized that producer cooperatives would be more efficient than conventional enterprises. That is, given the same physical resources, the producer cooperative would produce more than a comparable capitalist enterprise. The higher degree of efficiency in the cooperative arises because worker-members share in ownership and surplus earnings, have voting rights, and therefore are motivated to police the work effort of one another and to apply social pressure to those who shirk their work duties, feel a sense of loyalty and moral obligation to the group to put forth maximum effort in improving productivity, and can be given sufficient autonomy to exercise their skills to the fullest in solving problems related to production efficiency. The questions to be addressed in this section are whether producer cooperatives in fact operate more efficiently than conventional enterprises, and, if so, why? Since neither question is easy to answer definitively, the conclusions presented below must be viewed as tentative. The procedure will be to consider the English, French, Italian, American, and Basque cooperative histories, in that order.

The British Experience

The British producer cooperative movement documented by Derek Jones had its roots in the consumer cooperative movement and experienced its period of most substantial growth after the splitting off from the larger consumer cooperative organization in 1881 (D. Jones 1975, 1982a; Jones & Backus 1977; Oakeshott 1978, 52–73). Between 1881 and 1893 the number of producer cooperatives in England and Wales, many of which were associated with the newly formed Cooperative Production Federation, increased from 13 to 113. Even though the producer cooperatives formed their own separate organization, many still found their principal outlet for goods in the consumer cooperatives. After 1893 this group of cooperatives embarked upon a long period of slow decline to 16 enterprises in 1973 (Oakeshott 1978, 65). As Oakeshott points out, this pace of decline is remarkably slow, given the fact that a negligible number of new enterprises was created over the period. Of the enterprises that existed in 1913, 20 percent were still functioning 60 years later. To find a comparable level of performance for capitalist enterprises would be a difficult task.[4]

The structural principles of the British producer cooperatives include employee membership through the purchase of nominal share capital holdings, provision for employee participation in management, one vote per member, and the sharing of income by workers after materials costs and nominal interest costs on share capital have been paid.[5] There are, however, members who are not employees, and employees who are not members. Consequently, not all employees are able to participate fully in democratic decision making, and not all participants in decision making are employees (Oakeshott 1978, 67–68).

The question of comparative efficiency of British producer cooperatives relative to conventional enterprises in the same industries has not really been addressed. One study of matched pairs of capitalist and cooperative enterprises indicates that there is little difference in output per worker for the footwear industry and that the output per worker is higher for capitalist firms in other industries (Stephen 1984, 147–48). However, no conclusions can be drawn about relative X-efficiency because capitalist firms tend to have higher investment levels per worker. In a study of just the producer cooperatives, Derek Jones does, however, conclude that participation in decision making and surplus sharing increases output per worker. He finds that surplus sharing has a positive effect on output per worker in small producer cooperatives in the footwear industry and in all cooperatives in other industries, irrespective of size. He also finds surplus sharing to be dysfunctional for large footwear cooperatives, and that in all other cases it has a positive effect on productivity independent of the extent of employee participation. In addition, participation measured as the proportion of the board of management that is worker-members is positively associated with output per worker; and in co-operatives with a high level of this type of participation, the proportion of worker-members has a positive effect on output per worker (Jones 1982a, 193–94). While there is no evidence that British producer cooperatives are more X-efficient than their capitalist counterparts, there is some evidence that surplus sharing, participation in management, and sharing in ownership by workers has a positive effect on productivity.

The French Experience

While British cooperatives have survived in the marketplace for long periods of time, producer cooperatives as a group in England have experienced slow but steady decline, as already noted. By contrast, producer cooperatives as a group in France have a long history of steady growth in numbers. Although the roots of the French cooperative movement can be traced back to the 1830s, enduring success was not experienced by worker cooperatives until the turn of the 20th century. Between 1901 and 1975 the number of cooperatives grew steadily from 119 to 537, and in 1975 cooperatives as a whole employed around 30,000 workers (Oakeshott 1978, 123, 128). The French cooperatives are concentrated heavily in construction, engineering, and printing, and more than 50 percent employ fewer than 15 workers. The relative success of construction cooperatives can be explained partly by the low capital requirements and favorable treatment received from the French government in bonding requirements (Oakeshott 1978, 124). Even though the vast majority of cooperatives are small, there is a relatively large group of middle-sized cooperatives employing from 50 to 300 workers and 5 large cooperatives employing from 500 to 4,000 workers. One of the five is a major producer of telephone equipment, another is a leading producer of copper wire, a third is a large bottle producer, and the other two are major construction enterprises. Each is considered to be a leader in its field (Oakeshott 1978, 130–31). A common characteristic of most of the French cooperatives is that they were started by individuals of working-class background and historically have mistrusted professional management, although the more successful cooperatives have hired professional managers from outside (Oakeshott 1978, 138).

The organizational and property structures of the French producer cooperatives are defined in broad outline by French law. Although there is no formal requirement that workers must be members, two thirds of the board of directors must be workers. Shares in a cooperative must be sold at a nominal price,and the return on capital must be limited to 6 percent. Workers, whether members or not, share in profits; and the amount of profits going to workers must be at least as large as the total amount paid to shareholders (Oakeshott 1978, 141; Batstone 1982, 103). Nonworkers may hold shares, and all voting is on a one member, one vote basis, regardless of the number of shares held.

A study of the relative efficiency of cooperatives and conventional enterprises was undertaken for a sample of conventional and cooperative enterprises engaged in construction and printing in the Paris area (Batstone 1982, 106–16). This study concluded that value added per unit of labor cost was higher in cooperatives than in the industry as a whole in construction and printing. The cooperatives thus had a higher degree of X-efficiency than the industry as a whole, since they also had a lower level of capital investment per worker and a higher cost per worker than the industry as a whole. The cooperatives were also characterized by a higher value added as a percent of production and a higher ratio of value added to the net value of capital. Batstone argues that higher efficiency levels in cooperatives can be traced to fewer management personnel, greater worker motivation, and a higher skill level among workers, and indicates that interviews with workers suggest a high level of morale that can be traced to interesting work, a good atmosphere, good management-worker relationships, and good team spirit (Batstone 1982, 111, 113).

The Italian Experience

Although the Italian cooperative movement has been largely ignored in the academic literature, it appears to be the largest and one of the most dynamic on the European continent. According to one estimate, there were 2,675 producer cooperatives in Italy in 1977, employing approximately 147,500 workers.[6] As in England and France, the Italian producer cooperative movement has its historical roots in the latter half of the 19th century. The number of cooperatives associated with the major cooperative organization (Lega) increased from 68 in 1896 to 4,302 in 1921 (Oakeshott 1978, 148). From this point until the end of World War II, the cooperative movement was suppressed by the fascists and the major cooperative organizations were outlawed.

With reestablishment of the cooperative organizations after the war, the privileges the building and engineering cooperatives had held before the war in government contracting were reinstated, and new tax breaks and low-interest loans for cooperatives were added.[7] From 1951 to 1972 the cooperative movement in Italy was essentially stagnant, with little change in the total number of cooperatives (Zevi 1982, 240). However, over the period 1972–79 there was significant, steady growth in the number of cooperatives and cooperative employment. Over half the cooperatives are concentrated in the building industry, and a number of them are relatively large.[8] There is nonetheless a substantial and growing group of cooperative manufacturing enterprises producing building materials and some industrial goods (Zevi 1982, 241; Oakeshott 1978, 160).

The structure of the Italian cooperatives is similar to the French, except for a more stringent membership requirement. In general, workers must be members and only a limited number of outside shareholders is permitted. The cost of shares is nominal, although this varies to some extent from cooperative to cooperative. At least half of the profits must be distributed to workers directly or to accounts beneficial to workers. A minimum of 20 percent of any surplus earnings must be allocated to a reserve account, and a maximum of 5 percent interest can be paid in capital shares. The final governing body is the assembly of all workers, in which each worker has a single vote. The assembly elects a board of directors, and approves budgets and profit distribution plans.

The performance of a group of large Italian cooperatives has been studied and compared with that of similar capitalist enterprises in the construction and manufacturing sectors. In the case of the construction producer cooperatives, value added per worker was about 14 percent below that in capitalist construction enterprises. However, the capital-labor ratio of producer cooperatives was around 39 percent less than that for capitalist enterprises, which suggests that overall factor productivity was greater for the producer cooperatives. A similar pattern was found for manufacturing (Zevi 1982, 245–46). This provides tentative evidence that Italian producer cooperatives are more X-efficient than their capitalist counterparts.

The U.S. Experience

The U.S. producer cooperative experience is difficult to summarize because there has never been any central federation or government agency that has systematically collected and published data on cooperatives. Derek Jones, the only scholar who has attempted to trace the history of producer cooperatives in the United States, estimates that 785 producer cooperatives were established between 1790 and 1959 (D. Jones 1984, 38). Although many of these producer cooperatives had a fleeting existence, several clusters of them survived for some time, including foundry and cooperage cooperatives formed in the latter half of the 19th century, shingle weaving cooperatives started between 1910 and 1920, and plywood cooperatives formed between 1920 and 1960.[9] The life span of the approximately 47 cooperage cooperatives founded between 1840 and 1900 ranged from 1 to 24 years, with an average of slightly less than 10 years. The 16 cooperage cooperatives started between 1860 and 1900 experienced a life span ranging from 1 to 53 years, with a 12-year average. The shingle cooperatives lasted from 1 to 27 years, with a 10-year average life span; and of the 32 plywood producer cooperatives formed since 1921, 17 still existed in 1978. The total market share for the plywood cooperatives has ranged from 10 to 20 percent since 1940 (D. Jones 1982b, 61). While the cooperative movement has never been large, and has been characterized by significant growth for only brief periods, producer cooperatives have evidently been able to endure for relatively long periods of time.

Because of the absence of a uniform cooperative law or model cooperative organization publicized by a central federation, the structure of cooperatives is more diverse in the United States than in Europe. While the foundry cooperatives often sold stock to individuals in the local community, the cooperage, shingle, and plywood cooperatives restricted membership to workers. The use of nonmember-workers hired strictly for wages was very common in all cases. The plywood cooperatives made it a practice to hire managers who were not members. In the case of the cooperage, shingle, and plywood cooperatives, one member, one vote prevailed irrespective of share holdings. In the foundry cooperatives, however, voting was weighted by shares held. In all cases a board of directors was elected by the membership to oversee management of the enterprise. In contrast with the European cooperatives, the initial capital stake could be substantial, and in the case of the plywood cooperatives a share was marketable and brought a price as high as $35,000 (K. Berman 1967, 195). The plywood producer cooperatives distributed profits strictly in accordance with work performed by members, while the cooperage cooperatives distributed ordinary profits from production according to hours of work performed and extraordinary profits from gains in property value on an equal basis (D. Jones 1982b, 54–57).

Since the data on the 19th-century foundry and cooperage cooperatives are limited in availability, it is difficult to make judgments on their efficiency relative to conventional enterprises. However, Jones did find that productivity per worker in three of the foundry cooperatives was greater than the respective all-firm county averages. On the other hand, productivity for two cooperage firms was below county and state averages, although the data involved different years and the productivity level for one of the cooperatives was greater than the national average (D. Jones 1982b, 62).

More extensive research has been done on relative productivity of the plywood cooperatives. The Internal Revenue Service has accepted the principle of deducting the higher-than-industry-level wage rates paid to coop members in the calculation of corporate income taxes because audits have shown that the productivity is significantly higher in the cooperatives (K. Berman 1967, 166, 190). Two other studies have shown that output per worker is 25–40 percent greater in the producer cooperatives as a group than in the industry as a whole (K. Berman 1967, 189; Dahl 1956). A third study has concluded that variations in cooperative performance, as measured by the total return to the average worker-owner plus the net change in book value of a share, is significantly correlated to the extent of participation in management, as measured by an index that includes the percent of worker-owners who have served on the board or committees, the number of board meetings and general meetings, and the effectiveness of methods for distributing minutes of board meetings. Thus, a part of the explanation for superior performance is democratic participation (Belas 1972, 35–51).

The Spanish Experience

The single most successful example of regional cooperative economic development has occurred in and around the village of Mondragon in the Basque region of Spain. The Mondragon group of cooperatives started in 1956 with a single enterprise employing 24 workers, and by 1979 had grown to 70 industrial cooperatives employing 15,672 workers. In addition to the industrial cooperatives, a number of secondary cooperatives have been created, including a bank, a social security cooperative, a technical college, a research and development cooperative, education cooperatives, agricultural cooperatives, and service and con-

sumer cooperatives employing a total of 2,470 workers. The products
of the industrial cooperatives include refrigerators, ranges, automatic
washing machines, bicycles, capital equipment, tools, light engineering instruments, and electrical and electronic goods (Thomas 1982,
130–31).

A central figure in the founding of the Mondragon cooperatives
was Don Jose Maria Arizmendi, a parish priest appointed to Mondragon in 1941. He had studied Catholic social doctrine and was concerned with the economic problems facing Mondragon in the wake of
the fall of the Basque region to Franco in the Spanish Civil War
(1936–39). He was instrumental in establishing a technical training
school to provide local youth with industrial skills and instruction in
cooperative values. In 1956 five graduates of the school started an enterprise, Ulgor, to produce space heaters and gas ranges. Once legal
problems were worked out, Ulgor was converted to cooperative ownership. Over the years it has expanded and diversified its product
line, and by 1979 had reached an employment level of 3,855. While
Ulgor was the founding enterprise, the development of the cooperative system as a whole accelerated only after the establishment of the
cooperative bank, Caja Laboral Popular (People's Savings Bank).
As he had been in the case of the technical school, Don Jose Maria
was a key figure in the establishment of the bank, which began operation in 1960. Its purpose was to provide financial, technical, and
social assistance to cooperatives agreeing to a formal contract of association with the bank (Thomas & Logan 1982, 17–23, 46–47).

The structure of the Mondragon cooperatives is essentially the
same as that described above in Chapter 4. The Mondragon model
was chosen for the chapter on theory because it resolves many of the
problems faced by cooperatives, both theoretically and empirically.
Any cooperative that associates with the cooperative bank must agree
to abide by certain principles of employment creation, ownership,
earnings differentials, surplus distribution, and democratic organizational structure. Cooperatives are required to follow an open door
policy to the extent that "membership of the cooperative shall not be
restricted but shall be open to all those whose services are appropriate" (Thomas & Logan 1982, 24). While under this principle cooperatives can still limit membership, it does suggest a moral commitment
to employment creation. All members must make an initial capital
contribution that becomes a deposit in their individual capital accounts, on which interest is paid. A maximum of 70 percent of surplus

earnings in a given year is allocated to individual capital accounts, at least 20 percent of surplus earnings must go to a reserve fund, and 10 percent must go to a social fund for contribution to local projects of public value. Losses are borne at a similar ratio out of the reserve fund and individual capital accounts.

Since the individual capital accounts cannot be withdrawn until retirement or departure from the cooperative, 90 percent of surplus earnings remain within the cooperative group to be used for capital expansion. To foster solidarity among members, the maximum range of earnings differentials has been set so that the highest-paid member earns no more than three times the lowest-paid member. In addition, the average wage rate in the cooperatives is tied to the average pay level of major local capitalist employers. Surplus earnings are distributed to individual capital accounts in proportion to total wage and interest earnings of the individual workers. Consequently, surplus is distributed in accordance with current labor effort as well as past labor effort, since interest earnings will depend primarily upon the length of time one has been with the cooperative as well as upon the magnitude of past surplus distributions (Thomas & Logan 1982, 23-25, 131-61).

The contract of association not only lays down certain principles related to membership and ownership, but also requires that certain principles of internal organization be followed. Ultimate decision-making authority for a cooperative resides in the general assembly of all members, each of whom has one vote, and all workers in a cooperative must be members. Only in very exceptional circumstances can nonmember-workers be employed. While the general assembly can deal directly with important general policy issues, it elects a supervisory board that is charged with the task of selecting and overseeing the activities of management. Managers are appointed for a minimum period of four years and cannot be removed except for very serious incompetence. The responsibilities of management are those carried out by middle and top management in a conventional enterprise. The general assembly also elects a social council to deal with personnel matters and a watchdog council to audit the activities of management and the other councils (Thomas & Logan 1982, 24-29).

While the statistics for measuring the productive efficiency of the Mondragon cooperatives are of relatively high quality, good data for conventional enterprises in the Spanish economy are not as readily available. Nonetheless, Thomas and Logan were able to calculate a measure of value added per factor of production for both the cooperatives and Spanish industry, and found that for 1972 the figure was significantly higher for the cooperatives. They also were able to do a similar comparison for value added per person, and found the figure to be significantly higher for the cooperatives in four different years (Thomas & Logan 1982, 106–09). Although the evidence is not extensive, it does suggest that the Mondragon cooperatives are more X-efficient than their conventional counterparts.

While a direct empirical link cannot be drawn between higher X-efficiency and cooperative structure in the Mondragon group, there is evidence that members experience a high level of work satisfaction and approve of the cooperative structure of their enterprises. One measure of work satisfaction, absenteeism, has been found to be lower in Mondragon cooperatives than comparable capitalist enterprises (Thomas & Logan 1982, 49–52). Survey results indicate that workers perceive the most distinctive feature of the Mondragon enterprises to be their cooperative structure, that there is a high level of trust between management and workers in Mondragon cooperatives, that workers encourage one another to a greater extent in Mondragon cooperatives than in conventional enterprises, and that Mondragon workers strongly identify with one another and with their managers (Bradley & Gelb 1982, 155–60).

To summarize conclusions reached thus far, some producer cooperatives are apparently more X-efficient than their conventional counterparts. That is, out of a given set of physical resources, cooperatives are able to produce more output than conventional businesses. The apparent explanation for this is a higher level of worker effort in cooperatives.

Some economists have argued that cooperatives cannot be as efficient as capitalist enterprises because of shirking by individual workers (Alchain & Demsetz 1972). In a capitalist enterprise, capitalists receive the entire surplus generated by a reduction of shirking, and thus have a strong incentive to monitor work activity carefully in order to assure that shirking is minimized. Since surplus is spread across all employees in a cooperative enterprise there is little incentive for any single individual to adequately monitor shirking. The empirical evidence on productivity, however, suggests that there must be less shirking and greater work effort put forward in cooperatives relative to capitalist enterprises. Why is greater work effort forthcoming in a producer cooperative?

In Chapter 4 the argument was made that greater work effort and productive efficiency are forthcoming because of worker self-monitoring, individual worker identification with and moral commitment to the group as a whole, and the granting of greater autonomy to individual workers. As has been noted by others, workers in a cooperative will have a strong incentive to monitor their fellow workers to make sure they are not shirking. In a capitalist enterprise workers have no incentive to monitor their fellow workers because none of the surplus goes to them (Levin 1982, 46). As noted above, in the Mondragon cooperative group workers seem to encourage each other to a greater extent than do workers in conventional businesses. Self-monitoring of worker performance also takes place in the plywood cooperatives discussed above (Greenberg 1984, 198).

While worker self-monitoring is a likely outcome of worker ownership, worker identification with the organization as a whole, and the resulting individual commitment to efficient production, is the consequence of both ownership and participation in democratic decision making. The level of labor productivity has been found to be correlated to participation in decision making for both the British cooperatives and the U.S. plywood cooperatives (D. Jones 1982a; Belas 1972, 35–52). In the case of the plywood cooperatives, a survey study indicates that worker effort is related both to ownership and participation in management (Greenberg 1984, 182–99). This study also found that cooperatives have fewer supervisory personnel than comparable conventional enterprises, and that workers have more freedom on the job to arrange the work as they see fit within the constraints of the technology employed.

Such autonomy is feasible when workers internalize the goals of the organization as a whole. It contributes to productive efficiency because workers on the job are likely to discover superior methods and, in the case of a cooperative, will have a strong incentive to implement them. To quote the survey study of the plywood cooperatives by Greenberg, "Filled with a sense of responsibility for the enterprise as a whole, they [the worker-members] work in a manner that is sufficiently diligent and responsible as to require little outside supervision" (Greenberg 1984, 198). In sum, workers in organizations that are employee-owned and that follow principles of employee self-management tend to exhibit a moral bond to the organization that results in greater employee effort and productive efficiency, and permits greater individual autonomy in the work place.[10] As emphasized previously, this moral bond is not the result of social pressure from fellow workers, but arises from a psychic identification with others in pursuit of a common end.

To conclude our discussion of the X-efficiency of cooperatives, something should be said about the conventional critique of the feasibility of effective management in cooperatives. The clearest statement of the problem was given by the Webbs in their early work on cooperatives: "The relationship set up between a manager who has to give orders all day to his staff, and the members of that staff who, sitting as a committee of management, criticize his action in the evening, with the power of dismissing him if he fails to conform to their wishes, has been found by experience to be an impossible one" (Webb & Webb 1921, 468). The history of the cooperative movement suggests that there is an element of truth in this. Workers in the French cooperative movement have exhibited an element of antipathy toward professional management, although that has begun to change in recent years (Oakeshott 1978, 138). In the U.S. plywood cooperatives, managers have expressed dissatisfaction with their lack of autonomy, and turnover of managers has been substantial, although it has slowed and some stability has occurred in more recent years (K. Berman 1967, 159–62; Belas 1972, 53–80). The Mondragon cooperatives seem to resolve the management continuity problem by appointing management to a four-year term. If serious management problems exist in the plywood and the Mondragon cooperatives, to this point they have not markedly damaged productive efficiency, given the evidence that cooperatives outperform similar capitalist enterprises.

RESPONDING TO ECONOMIC CHANGE

The claim was made in Chapter 4 that cooperatives in theory respond more effectively to major economic change in product markets and technologies than do bureaucratic corporations. Corporations often respond to declining markets by withdrawing capital and discharging workers, and using their capital to acquire businesses in industries with growing product markets. The result is uneven regional growth; economic decline takes place in the regions with aging industries while economic growth is experienced in regions with new industries. The goal of the cooperative, on the other hand, is to provide employment opportunities to an existing group of workers in a specific location. If a cooperative's product market declines, then it must seek out a new product that can be produced by the existing group of worker-members. While this may be true in theory, can cooperatives in practice respond to substantial changes in product markets and technologies?

An initial look at cooperative history does not provide a very encouraging answer to this question. The British cooperative movement gained a foothold in the printing, textile, and clothing industries in the 1890s and has experienced a slow, steady decline ever since. Only one of the cooperatives, Walsall Locks, has expanded and diversified its product lines (Oakeshott 1978, 67). Although the British cooperatives have generally failed to move into new product markets, they have been tenacious survivors. The cooperatives are older than their capitalist counterparts and have a high survival rate (Oakeshott 1978, 65–66).

The French cooperatives have experienced growth in recent years, but that growth has been concentrated in the construction industry, the historical starting point of the cooperative movement (Oakeshott 1978, 121–44). The one exception is the largest French cooperative, AOIP, a major producer of telephone equipment. This enterprise experienced growth from 1,500 employees in the mid-1950s to 4,000 in 1976, which suggests that it was able to keep up with technological change in an industry where change has been relatively rapid.

Italian producer cooperatives also have experienced relatively rapid growth in the construction industry and have branched out into other industries primarily through buyouts of enterprises that would otherwise have shut down. While they have been relatively successful at saving jobs in older industries, the Italian cooperatives have not expanded into rapid-growth industries with sophisticated technologies (Zevi 1982, 239–51; Oakeshott 1978, 143–64).

In the U.S. cooperative movement, there are no examples of cooperative enterprises shifting their product line in the face of declining markets. The cooperage cooperatives simply went out of business as their product market faded, and the same thing seems to be happening to the plywood cooperatives (D. Jones 1984). Although Katrina Berman notes that the plywood cooperatives have installed more modern equipment, she nonetheless argues that keeping abreast of new developments, entrepreneurial foresight, and a long-term view are not strong features of group decision-making processes (K. Berman 1967, 187, 211). She also suggests that the need for retraining and job reorganization that results from the adoption of new technology is likely to create friction among workers. On the other hand, the first plywood cooperative, Olympia Veneer, was a technological leader in the industry (K. Berman 1967, 85–92).

Although cooperatives have survived in specific industries for long periods of time, there is no evidence that they have been able to adapt effectively to substantial changes in markets or technologies in Britain, France, Italy, or the United States. Why? One obvious answer is that change requires capital, and cooperatives have always had great difficulty getting capital. There are other possible explanations as well. As Berman suggests, workers as a group may be averse to taking the risks associated with change and may typically take a short-run view. If cooperatives are dominated by older workers nearing retirement, there may be little interest in moving into new product lines. Finally, individual cooperatives may have insufficient resources to carry out the research needed to develop a new product or technology, or to undertake the retraining of workers needed to carry out a new system of production.

All of these problems appear to have been resolved in the Mondragon cooperative group. The cooperative bank provides the necessary capital to develop a new product or technology and undertakes the necessary research on new market opportunities in its business services section. The research and development cooperative keeps abreast of new technologies and helps individual cooperatives with their research problems. The technical college devotes extensive resources to retraining individual workers in new technologies. Up to 1982 all of the industrial cooperatives that had ever been started in the Mondragon group were still going concerns. This exceptional success rate, unmatched by capitalist enterprises, attests to the resiliency of the Mondragon cooperatives and their ability to weather economic turbulence, such as that experienced in the mid-1970s and early 1980s (Thomas & Logan 1982, 14–95; Oakeshott 1978, 207–14). Because of all these supporting institutions, the risk to the workers from moving into new technologies or product lines is substantially reduced. While cooperatives as independent entities have considerable difficulty coping with major economic changes, a group of cooperatives associated with an appropriate set of support institutions can deal readily and effectively with the problem of economic change. In terms of regional development, the central advantage of such a cooperative group over the conventional corporation is that the former has a responsibility to provide its employee-investors with continuous employment opportunities in a given locality, while the latter is responsible only to its stockholders.

COOPERATIVE CAPITAL INVESTMENT

Historically, the central problem faced by all cooperatives, other than the Mondragon group, has been limited access to capital and a limited incentive to invest earnings in capital projects. Cooperatives cannot draw upon equity capital from nonworkers without jeopardizing their cooperative structure, and conventional financial institutions have often been reluctant to provide debt capital to cooperatives. This forces cooperatives to rely primarily on their worker-members and on surplus earnings as sources of funds for capital investment. As noted in Chapter 4, worker-members may be reluctant to invest surplus earnings or personal savings in a cooperative because of the difficulty of capturing the full return on the investment, since the return is captured through surplus earnings; a departing worker who lacks a marketable share in the enterprise will not receive surplus earnings beyond the point of employment termination.

Studies of the British, French, and Italian cooperatives indicate that the level of capital investment per worker is less in the producer cooperatives than in comparable capitalist enterprises, which confirms the hypothesis that cooperatives will be undercapitalized (Jones & Buckus 1977; Batstone 1982; Zevi 1982). Both the French and the Italian cooperatives have provisions that assets must be donated to other cooperatives if an enterprise is liquidated and that a certain level of capital investment must be maintained. As noted in Chapter 4, such provisions discourage capital investment because the amount invested can never be recaptured through increased surplus earnings.

The U.S. plywood cooperatives, on the other hand, are structured so that the return on investment and the principal will be realized by the worker-owners. This is accomplished by permitting shares to be sold at a market-determined price that will reflect the future earning power of the enterprise. The problem with this type of capital structure is that entering workers may lack access to enough capital to buy out departing or retiring workers. If this is the case, then the temptation to sell the enterprise to a conventional buyer will be great for a cooperative with a work force dominated by individuals approaching retirement age. The marketable shares concept thus endangers the principle of cooperative ownership. Even though the plywood cooperatives have an adequate incentive structure for reinvestment, they have nonetheless been undercapitalized, but have survived and prospered in many cases despite this handicap (K. Berman 1967, 137). Part of the problem is possibly a low savings rate by workers and a short economic time horizon. Another problem has been inadequate initial capitalization stemming form the lack of access to outside equity capital.

The problem of access to financial capital has been largely resolved in the Mondragon group of cooperatives through the structure of the contract of association with the cooperative bank. While each individual cooperative member is required to make a significant capital contribution, the bulk of the capital for a new enterprise generally comes from the bank in the form of debt capital. The bank has as its source of loanable funds the capital accounts of the individual enterprises and the deposits of local savers. Since 90 percent of surplus earnings is allocated to either individual capital accounts or collective reserve accounts for each of the cooperatives, the cooperatives themselves have a significant potential for accumulating capital, and a portion of this capital must be made available to the cooperative bank according to the contract of association (Thomas & Logan 1982, 22, 75–95). In essence, the problem of a low savings rate by workers or a short investment time horizon is solved through the forced savings of surplus earnings. Individual worker-members receive a market rate of interest on surplus earnings allocated to their capital accounts, and cooperatives must pay a market rate of interest on funds borrowed from the bank. Consequently, the problems of worker-members not receiving the full return on their capital invested and not getting back their original investment are eliminated. Investments will be undertaken as long as their return fully covers the opportunity cost of capital.

There is still a potential problem of disagreement between young and old workers over the types of investment undertaken in the Mondragon system. Older workers will favor investment projects that add to surplus earnings in the near future, while younger workers may favor projects that bring larger surplus earnings in more distant years. One solution to this problem would be to allow individual worker shares to be marketable; but, as already indicated, this could cause the price of becoming a worker-member to be very high. A compromise solution would be to retain the individual capital accounts and permit memberships to be marketed. The price of a membership would reflect the future earnings potential of the enterprise less the net book value of its assets, while the net book value would be fully reflected in the individual capital accounts. Doing this would reduce the membership price below what it would be in the absence of individual capital accounts. In any case, there is no evidence of an investment allocation problem in the Mondragon group under the existing system. The relative level of investment by the cooperatives has been substantial. Cooperative investment as a percent of total provincial investment has risen from 16 percent in 1971 to 62 percent in 1977, and the percentage of gross value added invested by the cooperatives averaged 36 percent over the period 1971–79, compared with 8.4 percent for the provincial economy as a whole (Thomas & Logan 1982, 103–06).

A final potential problem faced by the Mondragon cooperatives is a significant withdrawal of capital when a large number of workers reach retirement age. A potential solution to this problem is to convert individual capital accounts into annuities, in order to slow the pace of capital withdrawal from the cooperative group. Bradley and Gelb have argued that the Mondragon model might be difficult to apply in other Western industrialized countries because of labor mobility (1982, 156–69). If there was a high labor turnover in a cooperative group, then the rate of capital accumulation in individual capital accounts would necessarily be less because of a high withdrawal rate. Bradley and Gelb presume that high mobility is the result of cultural rather than economic forces. If in fact labor mobility is the result of employment instability, then the creation of stable employment opportunities in cooperatives would reduce the degree of work force turnover.

COOPERATIVE GROWTH

Once established, a producer cooperative has only limited incentives to grow through an increase in its work force if its goal is to maximize income per worker-member. An additional worker will be added only if the addition to income net of the addition to nonlabor costs is at least as great as the current income per worker. If the price of output increases, income per worker under certain circumstances could be increased by reducing the number of workers employed. Do such limitations on the growth of individual cooperatives hold in practice? Do cooperatives employ fewer workers than comparable capitalist enterprises?

The evidence on this question is mixed and limited in availability. In his work on the British cooperative movement, Derek Jones found that producer cooperatives in the footwear industry experienced a reduction of the average number of people employed between 1948 and 1968, while the opposite occurred for capitalist firms in the industry.

In addition, the growth of average value added for producer cooperatives was generally less than for comparable capitalist firms. Jones also found that the producer cooperatives are undercapitalized relative to their capitalist counterparts (Jones & Backus 1977, 496–506). Unfortunately, it is impossible to determine whether the smaller size of the producer cooperatives is a result of explicit decisions taken by the worker-members not to grow, or whether the lack of growth is simply the consequence of being unable to raise an adequate amount of capital (Stephen 1984, 147–48). The inability to raise capital could in turn be the result of the inability of workers to capture the return on investment because of limited tenure with the enterprise, a low savings rate of surplus earnings by workers, or lack of access to adequate outside capital.

Investigations of the other cooperative movements do not reveal any strong evidence of attempts to limit individual cooperative size. The French and Italian cooperatives apparently are somewhat larger in terms of employment than their conventional counterparts (Batstone 1982, 114; Zevi 1982, 244). Both the French and the Italian cooperatives as a group have grown in recent years, but comparisons of growth rates between capitalist and cooperative ventures cannot be made. As already noted, the largest French cooperative has made significant additions to employment in recent years. The average employment of the Mondragon cooperatives also has grown significantly since 1956 (Thomas & Logan 1982, 46–47). Although each of these cooperative movements is in theory subject to the incentive to limit employment, none seems to have suffered because of it. As already noted in Chapter 4, cooperatives are collective institutions that set objectives through democratic decision-making processes. Cooperative members may well decide to sacrifice income for other goals, such as long-term retention of market share or employment creation. The Mondragon cooperatives have a stated goal of expanding employment opportunities for local workers that seems to have found wide acceptance among cooperative members (Thomas & Logan 1982, 23–24, 190–91).

The U.S. plywood cooperatives have not been included in this discussion of growth incentives because they allow nonmenber employees to be hired at the going market wage, much like a capitalist enterprise (K. Berman 1967, 148–53). In contrast with the British and French cooperatives profits are not shared with nonworker-members in the plywood cooperatives. The end result of this practice is potentially a reversion to something approaching a capitalist enterprise with two separate classes, one made up of worker-owners sharing in the profits, and another made up of workers who receive wages only and do not participate in collective decision making. While many of the cooperatives do maintain a high percentage of worker-members, some have expanded by adding large numbers of nonmembers to their work force. The first cooperative, Olympia Veneer, eventually lost its identity as a cooperative by purchasing shares from departing members and hiring nonmember employees. The existence of marketable shares and the ability to hire nonmembers provide a substantial incentive for reversion to capitalist ownership, particularly when the market for member shares is an imperfect one where current shareholders may not be assured of capturing the full present value of future earnings because potential purchasers have difficulty in financing the purchase of shares. This problem could be solved if there were a cooperative financial institution that would provide loans to new members to purchase shares.

Even if individual cooperatives face limited incentives to add employees, the growth problem would be overcome if there were a high rate of new cooperative formation. The forces behind new cooperative formation will be considered below in the section "Initial Organization of Cooperatives."

SCALE AND DEMOCRACY

Democratic decision making tends to work more effectively in relatively small, homogeneous groups than in large groups characterized by diverse interests. The sense of participation will be greater in a small group even where decisions are made by elected representatives, because contact with such representatives will be easier in a small group than in a large one. As was discovered in the Mondragon group, disruptive conflicts are more likely to arise in large cooperatives. The group's only real strike occurred in its largest cooperative, Ulgor, over the issue of pay rates for specific jobs (Thomas & Logan 1982, 35). One of the apparent causes of the strike was the size of the cooperative (3,250 members), which led to a breakdown of communications between the supervisory board and the membership. As a result of this experience, the size of subsequent cooperatives was limited.

Limiting the size of the enterprise can, in theory, result in the forgoing of economies of scale. In a system of cooperatives this can be

avoided, however, through contractual arrangements between cooperatives to share certain services, or through the formation of second-
tier cooperatives like the bank, the technical college, or the research
institute in the Mondragon group. The governing arrangement and the
capital structure in these second-tier institutions are somewhat different from those in the industrial cooperatives. The supervisory boards
include not only employees but also representatives of the industrial
cooperatives that are the recipients of the services of the second-tier
cooperatives, and the industrial cooperatives provide a portion of the
capital investment in the second-tier cooperatives. The amount of
surplus distributed to employees in the second-tier institutions is tied
to the average distribution in the industrial cooperatives (Thomas &
Logan 1982, 77). Through such arrangements the advantages of scale
can be achieved without significantly reducing the effectiveness of
democratic decision making. Another structure that is being attempted for the purpose of obtaining scale economies is the formation of
cooperative groups in the Mondragon system. Each group would be
composed of cooperatives having common interests and would be
governed by a general assembly made up of the supervisory boards
and managements of the individual cooperatives (Thomas & Logan
1982, 38). The problem of balancing democracy against scale seems to
have been adequately resolved in the Mondragon group through institutional arrangements that permit the sharing of services and functions by the individual cooperatives.

INITIAL ORGANIZATION OF COOPERATIVES

Since the surplus earnings of a capitalist enterprise accrue to the
entrepreneur and the initial investors in perpetuity, the incentive for
forming such an enterprise is substantial. In the case of a producer
cooperative, the surplus earnings are spread among all of the employees. In a relatively large cooperative this obviously reduces the incentive for any single individual or small group to undertake the task of
initially organizing a cooperative. Consequently, it is not surprising
that so few cooperatives have been organized in comparison with the
number of capitalist enterprises in existence. Nonetheless, history
demonstrates that under certain circumstances, individuals do take
the initiative to organize producer cooperatives. Under what conditions have cooperatives been brought into existence? What incentives
have led to the formation of cooperative enterprises?

Historically, cooperatives have been formed for a variety of reasons in a variety of circumstances. The formation of the British producer cooperatives toward the end of the 19th century coincided with the organizing of the Cooperative Production Federation as a body with an existence independent of the larger consumer cooperative movement. Nonetheless, some of the producer cooperatives came into existence specifically to serve expanding consumer cooperatives. Others were started as a consequence of strikes and dissatisfaction with prevailing conditions in capitalist enterprises. The existence of an active federation, and growing interest in cooperatives among working people going back to the original Rochdale experiment, must have played a major role in the rapid growth of producer cooperatives in the 1880s and 1890s (Oakeshott 1978, 59–64). After the turn of the century, however, few new producer cooperatives were started, and the long decline of the existing cooperatives began. Oakeshott attributes the lack of further producer cooperative development in part to the antipathy toward cooperatives expressed by the British Socialist movement and the trade unions (1978, 35–51).

French and Italian producer cooperatives, unlike the British, have their historical roots in small artisan cooperatives that arose primarily in the construction industries and were started primarily to preserve artisan independence. In both countries, cooperatives have been assisted by special privileges in contracting for public works, and in Italy cooperatives have received special tax breaks. A few of those artisan cooperatives have grown into relatively large enterprises, such as AOIP, the telephone equipment maker in France, which started as an artisan cooperative in 1896 and by 1976 had achieved an employment level of some 4,000 workers. In addition to the artisan cooperatives, more recently a number of cooperatives have formed as a result of the closure of capitalist enterprises. This is particularly the case in Italy, where Lega, the cooperative association with ties to the Communist Party, has been quite successful in converting dying capitalist enterprises to cooperative ownership. Both the French and the Italian cooperative movements experienced expansion in numbers of cooperatives and employment during the 1970s, a period of relative economic turbulence. Both movements thus seem to do better in a period of crisis, when workers of necessity are looking to alternative means to preserve their jobs (Oakeshott 1978, 121–64; Zevi 1982; Batstone 1982).

The U.S. experience in the organization of producer cooperatives parallels the British experience to the extent that the formation of U.S.

cooperatives has been characterized by a burst of activity followed by slow decline rather than continuous growth. For example, the cluster of Minneapolis cooperative cooperages experienced its greatest growth in the period 1877–86, when the demand for barrels from the flour industry was high, and slowly declined as the market for barrels diminished until the last of the group shut down in 1928 (D. Jones 1977, 297; Stephen 1984, 164). The plywood cooperatives experienced substantial growth in the 1950s and 1960s, and since then have seen their market share diminish in the industry (K. Berman 1967, 191–93). The first plywod cooperative, Olympia Veneer, was founded in 1921 by 125 shareholders. Two men who worked in a lumberyard were instrumental in organizing the mill and sold shares primarily to Scandinavians who possibly had previous exposure to cooperatives in their native country. After a lean first year, the plant was unusually successful, a success that can be traced in part to the cooperative's early leadership in plywood technology (K. Berman 1967, 85–92). Most of the plywood cooperatives were formed in a seven-year period after World War II and adopted many of the features pioneered by Olympia Veneer, including marketable shares, equal pay for worker-members, distribution of surplus through a year-end bonus, and the employment of some nonmember-workers, although the other cooperatives generally did not follow Olympia's example of shifting almost entirely to a nonmember work force (K. Berman 1967, 92–94).

These plywood cooperatives were formed by workingmen or by promoters for the purpose of personal gain, and involved either the construction of a new facility or the conversion of an existing facility to worker ownership. In at least two cases, plywood cooperatives were formed as the result of efforts by groups of local citizens. The early 1950s was a period of growth for the plywood industry and of substantial speculation in shares for worker-owned companies. Promoters made their money from selling shares at a large profit, from fees, and from commissions on stock sales. In some cases, companies started as promotions were not properly structured or capitalized, and subsequently experienced difficulties. The promoters obviously were not concerned with the long-term health of the enterprises they established. Some cooperatives also had difficulty when workers bought out existing companies and paid too high a price or devoted too much of their capital to the initial purchase, leaving insufficient resources for working capital or modernization. Many of the plants that workers took over were old and unprofitable (K. Berman 1967, 104–28). Despite these problems, most plants were successful, and the cooperative plywood sector experienced significant growth up to the 1960s.

The Mondragon cooperative group provides the single most successful example of rapid and continuous creation of new producer cooperative enterprises, and its success in new enterprise creation can be attributed largely to the structure of the bank and the operation of its management services division. The central purpose of the bank is to provide credit to its associated cooperatives; it is legally limited to making outside investments in government-approved bonds that yield a low rate of return. Consequently, the bank must rely on the group of associated cooperatives as an outlet for its lending activity, and thus has a considerable interest in the growth of the cooperative group (Thomas & Logan 1982, 79–80). The bank manifests this interest through the activities of its management services division. The basic function of this division is to provide management services to existing cooperatives and, more important, to promote the establishment of new cooperatives. It carries out its functions with a staff of 150, including experts in business promotion, engineering, personnel, research, town planning, industrial buildings, and accounting.

The process of forming a new venture begins when a group desiring to form a cooperative comes to the bank (Ellerman 1984; Oakeshott 1978, 206–11). The group may have a product idea, or else it can draw upon a library of product prefeasibility studies maintained by the division. A manager is selected, a loan is arranged for the manager's salary during the period the feasibility study is being undertaken, and the manager works with a member of the staff on a lengthy and detailed project feasibility study that can take up to two years to complete. If the bank decides to go ahead with the project, capital financing is arranged and the production facility is constructed. Loan payments are deferred until the new cooperative is experiencing a positive cash flow, and the division staff member continues to work with the manager until the enterprise is on its feet. Of all the industrial cooperatives started through the management services division, only two have been shut down, and those closings occurred in the depths of the 1983 recession. Given that the failure rate for small businesses started in the United States is somewhere between 80 and 90 percent in the first five years, the success rate of the management services division is remarkable (Ellerman 1984, 288–89). As Ellerman suggests, the Mondragon cooperative group has successfully institutionalized the entrepreneurial function for the first time in a Western industrialized society.

CONCLUSION

The history of the producer cooperative movement clearly suggests that cooperatives have significant advantages as vehicles for carrying out regional development when they are structured in groups with appropriate supporting institutions. There is significant evidence that cooperatives in general, and the Mondragon cooperatives specifically, are more efficient than their capitalist counterparts. Once established, cooperatives are locationally stable and are tenacious survivors. Even without outside capital support, some have been technological leaders in their field.[11] Although cooperatives in isolation haven't always responded very well to economic change, it is clear in the Mondragon group, where supporting institutions are in place, that cooperatives are capable of keeping abreast of changes in technologies and markets. Cooperatives are responsible for maintaining economic opportunities for their worker-members, and thus have a strong interest in maintaining employment opportunities in a given locality. A cooperative bank required to invest in cooperatives will have a strong interest not only in maintaining employment opportunities in a given locality, but also in expanding them so as to have a growing outlet for its loanable funds. All this suggests that an appropriately structured system of cooperatives could go a considerable distance toward diminishing the downside of the long wave discussed in the first part of this book.

The history of the cooperative movement indicates that a central problem faced by cooperatives has been inadequate capital investment. Cooperatives have had trouble surviving because they have been undercapitalized. The problems of capital, growth, achieving appropriate scale without sacrificing democratic principles, and initial organization are all resolved through the formation of a system of cooperatives modeled after the Mondragon group. As already noted, the problem of initial organization is perhaps the most significant one for cooperatives and provides the largest barrier to cooperative development. Historically, cooperatives have been started by small groups of artisans desiring to maintain their independence, by workers faced with strikes or plant shutdowns, by groups of workers subscribing to cooperative ideology, and in some cases by cooperative federations and private promoters. All of these efforts have yielded a relatively small cooperative movement. The best prospect for cooperative development occurs when there is a support institution with a strong interest in the growth of a cooperative sector that is capable of institutionalizing the entrepreneurial function. The central question remaining to be answered, then, is the following: How, in the regions of the United States experiencing a retardation of economic growth, can the creation of financial and other support institutions be fostered that will in turn develop a cooperative economic sector?

NOTES

1. Much of the discussion that follows is based on a summary of the cooperative movement found in Gottlieb 1984, 129–48. Discussions of the limited cooperative activity that existed before the Rochdale Pioneers can be found in ibid., 129–30; Webb 1891; B. Jones 1894; and Knapp 1969, 5–28.

2. The larger membership could be attracted by patronage dividends or lower prices. Patronage dividends are not a necessary feature of successful cooperative retailing. They are useful, however, as an indirect means of raising capital, to the extent that members can be convinced to convert their dividends into stock in the cooperative.

3. For a descriptive history of the cooperative movement in U.S. agriculture, see Knapp 1969. For an account of the rural populist movement, see Goodwin 1976.

4. Apparently in the United States, nine of ten businesses fail in the first ten years (Pierce & Steinbach 1981, 4).

5. Some of the surplus is paid out as patronage dividends to customers and as dividends to shareholders (Jones & Backus 1977, 490–91, and 1982a, 179–80).

6. These data are not as reliable as they could be (Oakeshott 1978, 146; Zevi 1982, 240).

7. Retained profits may be exempt from, or subject to reduced rates of, corporate and local income taxes, depending on the relative size of total salaries and wages compared with all other costs (Zevi 1982, 242). Cooperatives do not have to put up bonds on public construction projects or go through competitive bidding with public authorities (Oakeshott 1978, 150).

8. The largest employs more than 3,000 workers (Oakeshott 1978, 159; Zevi 1982, 241).

9. The other groups of cooperatives considered by Jones include the Knights of Labor cooperatives, which were not very successful; two general categories of cooperatives; reforestation cooperatives started in the 1970s; and refuse collection cooperatives. The latter two groups appear to be relatively successful.

10. For another example, see Long 1978.

11. Olympia Veneer in the U.S. plywood industry and the French telephone equipment cooperative are two examples.

6

FOSTERING REGIONAL DEVELOPMENT: CREATING A COOPERATIVE ECONOMIC SECTOR

Once a cooperative financial institution comparable with the Mondragon bank is established, the collective goods problem in creating cooperative business ventures is to a large extent resolved. In order to have an outlet for loans, the bank must stimulate the development of new cooperative enterprises. It can accomplish this by providing extensive assistance to groups that wish to establish cooperatives and by providing initial seed capital. As a result, the risk of participating in the founding of a new enterprise is dramatically reduced, thereby increasing the incentive for potential founders of new businesses to approach the bank for capital and assistance. While the founders would not be able to capture an inordinate share of surplus earnings for themselves, they would likely occupy the better-paid managerial positions and would gain the satisfaction of successfully starting a business without having to face the high probability of failure that is common for new capitalist enterprises.

While the problem of starting new enterprises is effectively resolved, the question of establishing the cooperative financing institution in the first place still needs to be addressed. Who will start a regional cooperative-development financing institution? Where will the initial capital come from? How should such a financing institution be structured? What other support institutions are needed to ensure that cooperative economic development will be successful? Before addressing these questions directly, it is useful to consider the founding of the Mondragon financing institution briefly, and certain other forms of nontraditional economic development financing that have emerged in the United States.

THE FOUNDING OF MONDRAGON

The founding of the Mondragon group of cooperatives and the bank, Caja Laboral Popular, cannot really be addressed without considering the history and role of Don Jose Maria Arizmendi. Don Jose came to Mondragon in 1941 as the parish priest, a position he retained until his death in 1976. The Spanish Civil War had gravely damaged the local economy and had decimated a generation of community leaders. Don Jose sought to use his knowledge of economics and Catholic social teaching to restore prosperity to the local area, and to generate new leaders by focusing his efforts on the training of the young. By 1943 he had persuaded the local population to establish a technical training school where industrial skills would be taught to the local youth, and where students would learn about the principles of cooperation. As already noted, several of the graduates of this school went on to found the first cooperatives in Mondragon. When the early cooperators had exhausted their own capital resources, and when additional resources were needed for further growth of the movement, Don Jose suggested that a cooperative credit institution be established, having already done extensive research on its structure and feasibility (Thomas & Logan 1982, 17–23; Ellerman 1984).

The founding of the Mondragon group and its cooperative bank was thus the result of the efforts of an individual who had virtually no economic stake in the development effort. Although Arizmendi's role in the establishment of the Mondragon system cannot be minimized, the efforts of many others were involved, particularly those who established the first cooperatives. Rather than founding cooperative ventures, these individuals could have done better financially by creating capitalist enterprises. This suggests that the Basque "associative spirit" and basic egalitarian values can partly explain the early success of the Mondragon cooperatives (Guttierrez-Johnson & Whyte 1977). While ethnic values played some role in the initial establishment of the Mondragon cooperatives, their ongoing success cannot necessarily be attributed to ethnic solidarity. In their survey, Bradley and Gelb found that both Basque and non-Basque cooperators agreed that the distinguishing feature of the Mondragon enterprises is their cooperative nature rather than their Basque-ness (Bradley & Gelb 1982, 159). Once established, cooperative institutions can thus instill and perpetuate the appropriate values. The problem is that in order to get such institutions established in the first place, those who carry out the initial tasks of organization will have to be motivated by more than pure material gain.

ECONOMIC DEVELOPMENT FINANCE
IN THE UNITED STATES

While the popular conception of our own cultural heritage is one of extreme economic individualism, movements founded on strong communal values are not unknown in U.S. history. Examples include late-19th-century rural populism, an agricultural cooperatives movement, the labor union movement, and the community development movement of the 1970s and 1980s. Out of some of these movements have arisen unconventional organizations and financial institutions with the goal of fostering economic development. These institutions include agricultural credit cooperatives, community development corporations, community development credit unions, community banks, and state-level community-development finance authorities.

The most substantial precedent for initial government involvement in the establishment of cooperative credit institutions is found in the U.S. agricultural sector. Beginning in the 1930s, the rural cooperative movement had gained enough political influence to obtain legislation that over a 50-year period has established a network of farmer-controlled financial institutions (Gottlieb 1984, 142–43). While these institutions were initially aided with government loans, government capital contributions have been repaid and replaced over the years with equity drawn from shareholders and from the accumulation of reserves. These institutions as a group had outstanding mortgage and medium-term loans of $35.6 billion to approximately a million farm establishments in 1977.

Other examples of unconventional economic development and financing institutions can be found in the community development movement (Booth & Fortis 1984, 347–52). A community-based economic development movement with members professing communal values has emerged since the mid-1960s in a number of economically deprived localities and neighborhoods. Where private-sector businesses have found it insufficiently profitable to provide enough jobs, adequate housing, and sufficient commercial facilities, community organizations have in a number of instances attempted to fill the gap. Many such development efforts have been carried out through community development corporations (CDCs) or similar organizations that serve specific geographic areas under the direction of community-elected boards. The concept of a CDC had its origins in Philadelphia's black community and Rev. Leon Sullivan's 10-36 plan, in which church members contributed $10 for 36 months toward community economic development. These funds were channeled to a holding company, Zion Investment Associates, that undertook investments in a variety of enterprises in Philadelphia's inner city. This effort was representative of a long tradition of group-oriented development projects based on solidarist principles among blacks in the United States (Stewart 1984).

CDCs have been involved in housing development projects, the creation of community-owned and privately owned businesses, the development of commercial strips and shopping centers, and the delivery of social services. The key functions of the CDC in business development have been to search out entrepreneurs willing to start enterprises, help develop business plans, arrange for the capital financing of development projects, provide management consulting services, and plan (and sometimes undertake) physical improvements needed for economic development. The sources of funding for CDC staff and services include community memberships and other local fundraising efforts, government agencies, and foundations. CDC-sponsored business ventures have received debt and equity capital and grants from many of these same sources, as well as debt capital from local financial institutions.[1]

The success of the community development movement has been mixed and is difficult to evaluate. Many businesses started under CDC auspices are still operating successfully, but a good many have failed. The data on CDC development efforts are too limited to draw any conclusions on the relative performances of CDC and private-sector businesses. Since the failure rate for new private businesses is high—an estimated six out of ten in the first five years and nine out of ten in the first ten years—a relatively large number of failures for CDC ventures does not provide conclusive evidence one way or the other on the relative success of the community development movement[2] (Pierce & Steinbach 1981, 4).

Whatever the level of performance relative to the private sector, community-based enterprises have had to overcome substantially greater difficulties than private-sector ventures. CDCs operate in low-income localities and neighborhoods that are poor local markets for commercial businesses. Business development in such areas is hampered by a poorly educated local work force lacking basic work skills. Given these difficulties, the absence of manufacturing facilities that can accommodate modern production methods, and poor local access to transportation systems, CDCs frequently have difficulty attracting competent entrepreneurs and managers. CDC boards and staffs often lack the skills required for good project evaluation and selection. Perhaps one of the most significant problems faced by CDCs is the raising of funds to support staffs and to invest in venture developments. Before federal government funding for CDCs was recently eliminated, many CDCs depended on the Office of Economic Opportunity, and later the Community Service Administration, for funding and were therefore subject to changing bureaucratic whims on the types of projects to be undertaken and on the performance standards required for continued funding.[3]

The community development movement has spawned other institutions in addition to the CDC, including state-level community-development finance agencies, a community development bank, and community development credit unions. The first of the community-development financing agencies, the Massachusetts Community Development Finance Corporation (CDFC), was formed in 1978. The CDFC is a development bank that was initially financed through an issue of $10 million in general obligation bonds by the Commonwealth of Massachusetts. The purpose of the corporation is to make equity investments in businesses that are at least partly controlled by a CDC and located in a low-income community. The investment decisions are to be made by a nine-member board that includes three of the governor's state cabinet secretaries, two individuals experienced in investment finance, three CDC members who live in eligible target areas, and one representative of organized labor. The board also hires a president, who oversees the activities of the corporation's staff. The expenses of the staff are financed from the interest earned on the investment of a portion of the initial capital in government securities.

The creation of the corporation was primarily the result of political pressure from a group of community activists who recognized the need to have access to capital in order to gain control over the economic destiny of their respective communities (Sussman 1980). The corporation is able to make relatively long-term investments because the debt servicing costs on the original $10 million capital investment by the state come out of general state tax revenues rather than the earnings of the corporation (Litvak & Daniels 1979, 114–17). Even though the corporation does not have to pay the opportunity cost of its capital, it still has an incentive to make prudent investments to assure its own long-term survival, since it is unlikely to get a second capital allocation from the state.

A second community-development financing agency has been started in Wisconsin. The Wisconsin Community Development Finance Authority (WCDFA) has the same basic goals as the Massachusetts agency, but its capital and organizational structures are somewhat different (Fortis 1982). The Finance Authority is a nonprofit corporation that provides technical assistance and small venture development grants to CDCs desiring to start businesses in their local areas. It is governed by a board of directors that includes representatives from the Wisconsin State Department of Development, CDCs, organized labor, small businesses, employment and training programs, and the financial community. Debt and equity investments will be made by a separate entity, the Community Development Finance Company, under the guidance of the Finance Authority staff. Funding for the Finance Authority and capital for the Finance Company are provided by private-sector contributions and investments encouraged by state tax credits. A contribution to the tax-exempt Finance Authority is eligible for the normal federal and state tax deductions, and an investment in the Finance Company is subject to a 75 percent state tax credit. The Finance Company can also qualify as a small business investment company and a minority enterprise small business investment company in order to leverage its funds through the Small Business Administration.

The ties between the Finance Authority and the Finance Company are solidified by the Finance Authority's being a major stockholder in the Finance Company. One of the early problems faced by the Massachusetts Community Development Finance Corporation was an inadequate number of investment proposals from CDCs because of their lack of sophistication in business venture development (Kieschnick 1981a, 379). This problem is partially overcome in the structure of the Wisconsin agency by providing specifically for technical assistance and venture development grants directed at creating investment opportunities for the Finance Company. Both organizations potentially face a longer-term problem of cashing out of their investments in order to reinvest in newer ventures. Businesses started through CDCs are not likely candidates for public stock issues.

A second type of financing institution to emerge from the community movement is the community development bank. The single example of such an institution is the South Shore Bank in Chicago. It was acquired in 1973 by a bank holding company, the Illinois Neighborhood Development Corporation, and is one of four subsidiaries attempting to undertake comprehensive neighborhood development in the Chicago area. The objective of the bank is to combat neighborhood deterioration by providing credit to the residents of the South Shore area for the purpose of purchasing and improving single-family homes and multifamily rental buildings, starting and expanding small businesses, maintaining social services, and obtaining higher education. The other subsidiaries include City Lands Corporation, formed to acquire, rehabilitate, and sell residential and commercial properties; the Neighborhood Fund, a minority enterprise small business investment corporation licensed by the Small Business Administration to invest venture and development capital in neighborhood businesses; and the Neighborhood Institute, a nonprofit corporation that initiates social and economic development activities in the South Shore area (Grzywinski & Marino 1981, 251).

Still another institution that has evolved out of the community movement is the community development credit union (CDCU). A CDCU is a financial institution designed by federal law to increase the availability of financial capital to low-income communities. A recent study of a low-income neighborhood in the Chicago area found that residents had accounts in financial institutions totaling $1.8 billion, a surprisingly large amount, but that only around half of that sum was being returned to the community in the form of loans. The same study found that wealthier suburban areas received back a much higher percentage of their savings in the form of loans, which suggests that financial institutions funnel savings out of low-income areas in central cities (Caftel 1978, 1–16). Since the CDCU is a credit cooperative that must lend only to its members, who in turn must reside in a designated low-income area, savings deposits in a CDCU necessarily must remain in the local community. An eligible individual can join a CDCU through the purchase of a share draft (in conventional terminology, by opening a savings account). Each member is entitled to one vote, irrespective of the number of shares held, in the election of the board of directors and the credit committee that makes the final decision on loan applications (Caftel 1978, 35).

A CDCU can make real estate loans, mobile home and home improvement loans, personal loans (including business loans to individual members), and higher education loans. The limit on the amount it can loan to an organizational member is that member's total deposit. Although this in theory limits a CDCU's ability to make loans to organizations, such as cooperatives, CDCUs nonetheless have made personal and real estate loans to businesses, including cooperatives. There are approximately 150 CDCUs in existence, with an average of around 1,000 members and $600,000 in assets. The central problem faced by CDCUs is their small size and a loan loss rate that is somewhat higher than that of all credit unions as a group (Caftel 1978, 38, 42, 50–51).

REGIONAL COOPERATIVE DEVELOPMENT AND FINANCING

Although it is comparatively small, there is a group of financial and development institutions in this country that are based on either cooperative or community values. Some in this group, such as farm credit institutions, have been quite successful, while others, such as state community-development finance agencies, community development corporations, and community-development credit institutions, are still in their formative years and cannot at this point be easily evaluated. Nonetheless, such institutions are part of a tradition upon which a more extensive system of cooperative development and financing institutions can be built.

If a simple replication of the Mondragon bank and its associated cooperatives in the United States were feasible, little further discussion would be required. However, given the highly conservative nature of bank lending activity in this country, some modification of the Mondragon model will be required. When a new cooperative is being established in the Mondragon group, the cooperative bank makes a loan to the cooperative without requiring repayment until the cooperative achieves a positive cash flow. This type of loan is uncommon in the United States, where initial capitalization usually occurs through equity investment. Banks in this country simply do not make high-risk loans to new businesses without substantial collateral. Banks look upon potential borrowers with a low ratio of equity to debt capital as very high risks because of the lack of collateral arising from equity investment.

Banks engage in risk-averse behavior not only because of relatively conservative bank regulation, but also as a result of a high degree of banking concentration in local financial markets that primarily serve small businesses (Litvak & Daniels 1979, 48–50). Banks that have local market power often exercise it through minimizing average risk per loan rather than through charging higher interest rates on loans. In any case, it is difficult to imagine that bank regulators in this country would permit banks to make extensive deferred-payment loans that new cooperative businesses would require in their early years. Any new business needs a period of time to get established before positive cash flows can be generated to meet debt servicing payments.

Since it is unlikely that a banking institution in this country, even a cooperative one, would be able to provide seed capital for new cooperative ventures, the obvious alternative is to establish some sort of equity financing institution for cooperatives. To do so, however, could lead to a violation of the cooperative principle of worker-member control over the supervisory board if equity investment brings with it conventional voting rights. The solution to this problem is to establish nonvoting shares that would receive dividends based on some portion of surplus earnings. Also, provisions could be made for worker-members to repurchase outside shares after the business gets on its feet. To avoid potential exploitation of outside shareholders by workers, wage rates would have to be tied to prevailing market levels according to some clearly specified formula. Otherwise, worker-members could simply raise their wages to eliminate surplus earnings and payments to outside shareholders. To foster cooperative economic development, then, a cooperative venture capital fund can be established at the state level or in a metropolitan area that is large enough to provide sufficient investment opportunities. The purpose of this fund would be to make investments in nonvoting stock shares in producer cooperatives. The venture capital fund would also provide the technical assistance needed by new cooperatives through doing product feasibility studies and business plans, and could maintain a library of prefeasibility studies much as the business services division does for the Mondragon cooperative bank.

To assure that the stock of capital for investment would continue to expand, cooperatives assisted by the venture capital fund could be contractually required to deposit some portion of their member-workers' individual capital accounts with the fund. The venture capital fund could be organized as a second-degree cooperative with associated cooperatives being its members and, along with the fund's employees, electing the fund's supervisory board. The earnings distributed to the fund's employees could then be tied to the average surplus earnings of the affiliated cooperatives. The fund could also be responsible for assisting cooperatives that are having difficulties and directing them into new product lines if necessary. In short, the cooperative venture-capital fund could fulfill the role of the management services division in the Mondragon bank, and such a fund would be free of the restrictions on conventional banking. It would be charged with the task of stimulating the formation of new cooperative enterprises and assisting in the preservation of existing ones.

Although banks in this country are too conservative in their lending policies to stimulate new business formation, they do have distinct advantages in the evaluation of small business lending opportunities. Small businesses are caught in a bind between large-scale financial institutions and markets, and banks of an appropriate scale to serve their needs. Large financial institutions, such as insurance companies and investment banks, invest on a large scale in order to minimize the transaction costs involved in evaluating investment opportunities, and therefore usually ignore small business investment opportunities. In addition, new businesses simply cannot afford the large up-front costs of a public stock issue. Consequently, large financial institutions and equity markets are not readily accessible to new businesses, which are likely to be relatively small. On the other hand, local banks have developed skills in minimizing transaction costs for small-scale investments in small business, but are unwilling to risk their capital on new ventures (Litvak & Daniels 1979, 11–26, 36–57).

It would therefore make sense somehow to combine a cooperative venture-capital fund with a cooperative bank to take advantage of the skills the latter would gain in evaluating small business investments. This could be done by forming a cooperative bank holding company along the lines of the relationship between the Illinois Neighborhood Development Corporation and the South Shore Bank discussed above. A cooperative bank would also be needed if conventional lenders were unwilling to make conventional loans to established cooperatives with adequate collateral because of their untraditional ownership and organizational structure. The bank itself would be a conventional lending institution that is wholly owned by the holding company, which in turn would be structured as a second-degree cooperative owned and controlled by the associated cooperatives. Associated cooperatives would be requried to invest in the holding company by purchasing shares, using their individual capital accounts as the source of financing. Association would give a cooperative access to the services of both the venture capital fund and the bank.

Once a cooperative venture-capital fund and bank were established, would entrepreneurs in this country come forward to use their services? Would entrepreneurs be willing to give up individual control and accept the cooperative model in order to get the capital and assistance offered by the venture capital fund and bank? As suggested above, new business ventures have great difficulty raising seed capital. They have access neither to large financial institutions nor to conventional equity markets because of the relatively large transaction cost involved, and they lack access to unsecured capital from risk-averse local banks. This leaves personal wealth and venture capital companies as the sources of capital. Since only a few entrepreneurs are personally wealthy or have access to wealthy friends and relatives, and since only a small percentage of all new ventures are funded by venture capital companies, many new business ideas go untried (Litvak & Daniels 1979, 11–26, 36–57). Given these imperfections in the capital market, many entrepreneurs would likely be attracted to a cooperative venture-capital fund with its ability to substantially reduce the risk of new business start-ups.

If it turned out that a cooperative venture-capital fund was unattractive because of its restriction to funding cooperative enterprises, a compromise approach between pure capitalism and cooperation could be employed. The cooperative venture-capital fund would agree to invest in an enterprise controlled by the entrepreneur if the entrepreneur agreed to sell the business to the workers at fair market value after a specified period of time. One of the most difficult problems that entrepreneurs face in business ventures they start is being able to sell the enterprise, particularly if it is not large enough to be acquired by another firm or to be sold through a public stock issue. By selling the enterprise to the workers, the entrepreneur would gain a significant amount of the value resulting from the successful creation of the enterprise, and a producer cooperative would be created in the longer run. It is conceivable that such an approach may be required to introduce successful cooperative ventures into a society that strongly professes individualistic values.

Would workers in this country be willing to accept the retention of surplus earnings and the individual capital account structure that is such an important part of the Mondragon cooperative model? If wage rates are set at market levels, and if memberships are readily financed through payroll deductions, then few objections would likely occur, particularly if productivity, and therefore earnings, are greater in the cooperative than in the conventional enterprise. Also, the ability of cooperatives to satisfy nonmaterial needs should have some attraction for workers in this country. Bradley and Gelb mention one problem associated with worker mobility that must be resolved, however. They argue that in most industrialized societies, workers' movement from one job to another will result in excessive withdrawals of capital from individual capital accounts (Bradley & Gelb 1982). The problem may not be as significant as they suggest, given that much labor mobility is the result of capital movements and layoffs in industrialized economies lacking employment guarantees. However, if it does turn out to be a problem of some substance, it could be mitigated by requiring that capital account withdrawals be carried out over a specified period of time, or that withdrawals be made only after retirement age is reached, irrespective of place of employment.

The final, and most important and difficult, question that needs to be addressed is this: Who will initially organize and capitalize cooperative financial institutions? One possibility is a bootstrap effort by local communities around the country that have been hit hard by regional long-wave downturns. Community groups, church organizations, or labor unions concerned with deteriorating local economic conditions could organize financial institutions for the purpose of building up a local cooperative sector. This could be initiated, for example, through the purchase of a local bank or the creation or expansion of a community development credit union. The analysis of chapters 4 and 5 suggests that the performance of the community-based development movement can be improved through the adoption of cooperative principles and the support of cooperative ownership.

Cooperative, rather than individual, ownership of community-based enterprises would lead to higher levels of productivity and innovation, and would give the local economy a competitive edge in national and international markets. Workers who are also owners would have a substantial stake in the success of a new cooperative venture and thus would be more likely to put forth the work effort needed to keep it afloat in the critical early years than would employees of a conventional new business. Workers who have suffered from long periods of unemployment will be more willing to work for reduced wages in the startup phase, knowing that through ownership they will ultimately benefit from the success of the enterprise. Successful cooperatives in a community will generate pools of savings that are potentially available for further development efforts. Cooperatives organized on the Mondragon model could be required, for example, to invest a portion of their individual capital accounts in a cooperative venture capital fund and a cooperative bank. Successful cooperatives could also be required to allocate a portion of their surplus to community services and improvement projects. A final advantage of cooperative ownership is that, unlike private or corporate owners, workers who live in a given community and own a community-based business are unlikely to move that business out of the community (Booth & Fortis 1984, 348–49).

Since the benefits of cooperative financial institutions are collectively realized and shared, these institutions will require groups of socially motivated individuals to bring them into existence. Such institutions cannot exist in a vacuum, and must be the product of leadership and support from some broad-based social movement. This clearly was the case in the organization of the Mondragon group and its cooperative bank. Government also could play a central role in initiating a cooperative sector. Local, state, or federal government agencies could provide long-term loans for initial capitalization of a cooperative venture-capital fund and bank. These loans would have to involve deferred payment schedules in order to give the venture capital fund and the bank sufficient time to achieve an adequate cash flow. Alternatively, government agencies could make investments in nonvoting equity shares that would ultimately be repurchased by the cooperative venture-capital fund and bank. It is even conceivable that a highly entrepreneurial branch of government could create these financing institutions itself. If they are successful, government and the public in general would reap a substantial benefit in the form of an enlarged tax base and reduced social costs associated with unemployment.

A number of state-level financing agencies in venture development and housing have been successfully established (Litvak & Daniels 1979, 99–137). The great difficulty with government involvement in cooperative financial institutions is the potential for political influence on financial decision making. Funding of new ventures should be based on economic feasibility, not on political criteria. If politics plays an excessive role in such decision making, the financing institutions could well be doomed. The ideal situation would be for government simply to act as an investor in the cooperative financing institutions without demanding direct control. If the board of such financing institutions is made up of associated cooperatives, employees, and representatives of depositors or investors, then it is likely to be relatively broad-based and thus not to need to have board slots allocated to government agency heads or politicians, as is commonly the case in many quasi-government financing institutions.

RESEARCH AND DEVELOPMENT

In addition to cooperative financial institutions, a successful cooperative group is likely to require the services of a substantial research and development organization. The creation of the new technology and the new product has moved out of the machine shop and into the research laboratory. The research university is becoming an increasingly important center for the development of new technologies with commercial applications. In fact, universities themselves have become tools of regional development by engaging in the construction of research parks intended to foster technology transfers from university researchers to private enterprises. The function of such parks is to provide research and development facilities with easy access to university campuses and the consulting services of their faculties. The goal is to draw the university into product-development-related research that will benefit private businesses. The basic model for such facilities is the highly successful Stanford University Research Park, which played such an important role in the founding of the semiconductor industry in the area just south of San Francisco. The problem with this approach is that it draws the university faculty away from basic research, which is ultimately the foundation of technological progress.

A superior approach would be to establish research and development institutions separate from public universities that have as their central function the development of new products and new technologies. Such institutions could realize scale economies beyond the entrepreneurial ventures typically attracted to research parks, and would leave the university to concentrate on its basic research function. Such institutions could be organized as cooperatives, with the general assembly being made up not only of employees but also of the client enterprises. The budget for such institutions could come from grants from the client enterprises as well as from fees and royalties, and government research grants.

CONCLUSION

What are the prospects for a cooperative movement of substance in this country? Historically, cooperative movements have emerged when working people faced loss of employment during times of economic crisis or labor strife, or when there was a strong desire among working people for control of their own destiny. At the present moment in this country, many workers are faced with a crisis of unemployment, particularly in those regions confronted with the loss of aging industries. There has recently been a spurt in the growth of employee-owned enterprises, although for many of these, control has remained in the hands of management or major outside investors (D. Jones 1984, 39). If the crisis of unemployment continues and even deepens, a growing movement for cooperative development is conceivable. As already noted, the leadership of this movement could come from church groups, community organizations, and labor unions that see their traditional functions disappearing with the decline of older industries. If state and local governments in declining regions continue to experience fiscal difficulties and political pressure to resolve the unemployment problem, it is conceivable that government itself could take the initiative to create a major cooperative economic sector. Whether this will happen cannot be predicted on the basis of the material presented in this book. What this book does provide, however, is an alternative vision of an economy that can avoid the devastating consequences of regional long-wave downturns and employment depressions.

NOTES

1.   For early, somewhat optimistic descriptions of the community development movement and the community development corporation, see Faux 1971; Harrison 1974. For a sample of case study material on community-based economic development, see Stein 1976; Roberts et al. 1980, 103–25; Echeveste 1979; Garn et al. 1976; Berndt 1977.

2.   For one attempt to evaluate CDCs, see Garn et al. 1976. This report presents a genuinely mixed picture of successes and failures in three different community-based organizations. For a totally negative view of CDC accomplishments, see Berndt 1977. His analysis relies primarily on his own experience with community development in St. Louis.

3.   For critical analyses of community-based economic development and its problems, see Daniels et al. 1981; Michelson 1981; Berndt 1977.

BIBLIOGRAPHY

Alchain, A. A., and A. Demsetz. 1972. "Production, Information Costs, and Economic Organization." *American Economic Review,* December, pp. 777-95.

Alchain, A. A. 1950. "Uncertainty, Evolution, and Economic Theory." *Journal of Political Economy,* June, 211-21.

Batstone, Eric. 1982. "Country Studies: France." In *The Performance of Labor-Managed Firms,* Frank H. Stephen, ed., pp. 99-121. New York: St. Martin's Press.

Belas, C. J. 1972. *Industrial Democracy and the Worker-Owned Firm.* New York: Praeger.

Berman, Katrina V. 1967. *Worker-Owned Plywood Companies: An Economic Analysis.* Pullman: Washington State University Press.

Berman, Katrina V., and M. D. Berman. 1978. "The Long-Run Analysis of the Labor Managed Firm: Comment." *American Economic Review,* September, pp. 701-09.

Berman, Matthew D. 1977. "Short-Run Efficiency of the Labor-Managed Firm." *Journal of Comparative Economics* 1: 309-14.

Berndt, Harry Edward. 1977. *New Rulers in the Ghetto: The Community Development Corporation and Urban Poverty.* Westport, Conn.: Greenwood Press.

Birch, David L. 1979. "The Job Generation Process." Cambridge, Mass.: M.I.T. Program on Neighborhood and Regional Change.

Bluestone, Barry, and Bennett Harrison. 1982. *The Deindustrialization of America.* New York: Basic Books.

Bluestone, Barry, Peter Jordan, and Mark Sullivan. 1981. *Aircraft Industry Dynamics: An Analysis of Competition, Capital, and Labor.* Boston: Auburn House.

Booth, Douglas E. 1985. "Problems of Corporate Bureaucracy and the Producer Cooperative as an Alternative." *Review of Social Economy,* December, pp. 298-315.

———. 1978. *"The Differential Impact of Manufacturing and Mercantile Activity on Local Government Expenditures and Revenues."* National *Tax Journal,* March, pp. 33-52.

Booth, Douglas E., and Louis G. Fortis. 1984. "Building a Cooperative Economy: A Strategy for Community Based Economic Development." *Review of Social Economy,* December, pp. 339-59.

Borcherding, Thomas E., and Robert T. Deacon. 1972. "The Demand for the Services of Non-federal Governments." *American Economic Review,* December, pp. 891–901.

Bradley, Keith, and Alan Gelb. 1982. "The Mondragon Cooperatives: Guidelines for a Cooperative Economy?" In *Participatory and Self-Managed Firms,* Derek Jones and Jan Svejnar, eds., pp. 153–72. Lexington, Mass.: Lexington Books.

Burns, Arthur F. 1934. *Production Trends in the United States Since 1870.* New York: National Bureau of Economic Research.

Caftel, Brad J. 1978. *Community Development Credit Unions: A Self-Help Manual.* Berkeley, Calif.: National Economic Development Law Project.

Dahl, H. E. 1956. "Worker Owned Plywood Companies in the State of Washington." Everett, Wash.: First National Bank of Everett. Unpublished manuscript.

Daniels, Belden, Nancy Berbe, and Beth Seifel. 1981. "The Experience and Potential of Community-Based Development." In *Expanding the Opportunity to Produce,* Robert Friedman and William Schweke, eds., pp. 176–85. Washington, D.C.: Corporation for Enterprise Development.

Dugger, William M. 1985. "The Continued Evolution of Corporate Power." *Review of Social Economy,* April, pp. 1–13.

Dun and Bradstreet Corporation. 1950–82. "Monthly New Business Incorporations." New York: Economic Analysis Department, Dun and Bradstreet Corporation.

Echeveste, John A. 1979. "TELACU: Pioneers in Economic Development." *National Economic Development and Law Center Report,* March/April, pp. 31–33.

Edwards, Richard. 1979. *Contested Terrain: The Transformation of the Workplace in the Twentieth Century.* New York: Basic Books.

Ellerman, David P. 1984. "Entrepreneurship in the Mondragon Cooperative." *Review of Social Economy,* December, pp. 272–94.

———. 1983a. "A Model Structure for Cooperatives: Worker Co-ops and Housing Co-ops." *Review of Social Economy,* April, pp. 52–67.

———. 1983b. "Theory of Legal Structure: Worker Cooperatives." Somerville, Mass.: Industrial Cooperatives Association.

———. 1983c. "On the Labor Theory of Property." Somerville, Mass.: Industrial Cooperatives Association.

Faux, Geoffrey. 1971. *CDCs: New Hope for the Inner City.* New York: Twentieth Century Fund.

Fisher, Franklin M., James W. McKie, and Richard B. Mancke. 1983. *IBM and the U.S. Data Processing Industry: An Economic History.* New York: Praeger.

Fortis, Louis G. 1982. "Wisconsin's CED Program Promotes Private Sector Support." *Economic Development and Law Center Report,* Fall, pp. 8–10.

Furabotn, Eirik G. 1976. "The Long-Run Analysis of the Labor-Managed Firm: An Alternative Interpretation." *American Economic Review,* March, pp. 104-23.

Garn, Harvey A., Nancy L. Tovis, and Carl E. Snead. 1976. *Evaluating Community Development Corporations—A Summary Report.* Washington, D.C.: The Urban Institute.

Goodwyn, Lawrence. 1976. *Democratic Promise: The Populist Movement In America.* New York: Oxford University Press.

Gottlieb, Manuel. 1984. *A Theory of Economic Systems.* New York: Academic Press.

Greenberg, Edward S. 1984. "Producer Cooperatives and Democratic Theory: The Case of the Plywood Firms." In *Worker Cooperatives in America,* Robert Jackall and Henry M. Levin, eds., pp. 171-214. Berkeley: University of California Press.

Brzywinski, Ronald A., and Dennis R. Marino. 1981. "Public Policy, Private Banks and Economic Development." In *Expanding the Opportunity to Produce,* Robert Friedman and William Schweke, eds., pp. 243-56. Washington, D.C.: Corporation for Enterprise Development.

Gutierrez-Johnson, Ana and William Foote Whyte. 1977. "The Mondragon System of Worker Cooperatives." *Industrial and Labor Relations Review,* 31, October, pp. 18-30.

Harrison, Bennett. 1974. "Ghetto Economic Development: A Survey." *Journal of Economic Literature,* March, pp. 1-27.

Hekman, John S. 1980. "The Future of High Technology Industry in New England: A Case Study of Computers." *New England Economic Review,* January/February, 5-17.

Helyar, John. 1984. "Rexnord to Buy Maryland Firm." *Wall Street Journal,* December 11, p. 10.

Jenkins, David. 1973. *Job Power: Blue and White Collar Democracy.* Garden City, N.Y.: Doubleday.

Jones, B. 1894. *Cooperative Production.* Oxford: Oxford University Press.

Jones, Derek C., 1984. "American Producer Cooperatives and Employee-Owned Firms: A Historical Perspective." In *Worker Cooperatives in America,* Robert Jackall and Henry M. Levin, eds., pp. 37-56. Berkeley: University of California Press.

_____. 1982a. "British Producer Cooperatives, 1948-1968: Productivity and Organizational Structure." In *Participatory and Self-Managed Firms,* Derek Jones and Jan Svejnar, eds., pp. 175-98. Lexington, Mass.: Lexington Books.

_____. 1982b. "The United States of America: A Survey of Producer Cooperative Performance." In *The Performance of Labour-Managed Firms,* Frank H. Stephen, ed., pp. 53-73. New York: St. Martin's Press.

_____. 1977. "The Economics and Industrial Relations of Producer Cooperatives in the United States, 1791–1939." *Economic Analysis and Workers' Management* 11: 295–317.

_____. 1975. "Workers' Management in Britain." Ibid. 9: 332–37.

Jones, Derek C. and David K. Backus. 1977. "British Producer Cooperatives in the Footwear Industry: An Empirical Evaluation of the Theory of Financing." *The Economic Journal,* September, pp. 488–510.

Kieschnick, Michael. 1981a. "The Role of Equity Capital in Urban Economic Development." In *Expanding the Opportunity to Produce,* Robert Friedman and William Schweke, eds., pp. 374–86. Washington, D.C.: Corporation for Enterprise Development.

_____. 1981b. *Taxes and Growth: Business Incentives and Economic Development.* Washington, D.C.: Council of State Planning Agencies.

Knapp, Joseph A. 1969. *The Rise of American Cooperative Enterprise: 1620–1920.* Danville, Ill.: Interstate Publishers.

Kondratieff, N. D. 1935. "The Long Wave in Economic Life." *Review of Economics and Statistics* 17: 105–15.

Kress, Andrew J. 1941. *Introduction to the Cooperative Movement.* New York: Harper and Brothers.

Leibenstein, Harvey. 1966. "Allocative Efficiency vs. X-Efficiency." *American Economic Review,* June, pp. 392–415.

Levin, Henry. 1982. "Issues in Assessing the Comparative Productivity of Worker Managed and Participatory Firms in Capitalist Societies." In *Participatory and Self-Managed Firms,* Derek C. Jones and Jan Svejnar, eds., Lexington, Mass.: Lexington Books.

Litvak, Lawrence, and Belden Daniels. 1979. *Innovations in Development Finance.* Washington, D.C.: Council of State Planning Agencies.

Long, Richard J. 1978. "The Effects of Employee-Ownership or Organizational Identification, Employee Job Attitudes, and Organizational Performance: A Tentative Framework and Empirical Findings." *Human Relations* 31, no. 1: 29–48.

Maslow, Abraham, H. 1954. *Motivation and Personality.* New York: Harper & Row.

Mensch, G. 1979. *Stalemate in Technology.* New York: Ballinger.

Michelson, Stephan. 1981. "Community Based Development in Urban Areas." In *Expanding the Opportunity to Produce,* Robert Friedman and William Schweke, eds., pp. 534–49. Washington, D.C.: Corporation for Enterprise Development.

Norton, R. D. 1979. *City Life-Cycles and American Urban Policy.* New York: Academic Press.

Norton, R. D., and J. Rees. 1979. "The Product Cycle and the Spatial Decentralization of American Manufacturing." *Regional Studies,* 13, no. 2: 141–51.

Oakeshott, Robert. 1978. *The Case for Workers' Co-ops.* London: Routledge and Kegan Paul.

Olson, Mancur, Jr. 1983. " The South Will Fall Again: The South as Leader and Laggard in Economic Growth." *Southern Economic Journal,* April, 917–32.

_____. 1971. *The Logic of Collective Action.* New York: Schocken Books.

Pierce, Neal R., and Carol Steinback. 1981. "Reindustrialization on a Small Scale—But Will the Small Business Survive?" In *Expanding the Opportunity to Produce,* Robert Friedman and William Schweke, eds., pp. 4–9. Washington, D.C.: Corporation for Enterprise Development.

Plaut, Thomas R., and Joseph E. Pluta. 1983. "Business Climate, Taxes and Expenditures, and State Industrial Growth in the United States." *Southern Economic Journal,* July, pp. 99–119.

Roberts, Benson F., Robert O. Zdenek, and William E. Rivens. 1980. *Community Development Corporations and State Development Policy: Potential for Partnership.* Washington, D.C.: National Congress for Community Economic Development.

Rostow, W. W., and M. Kennedy. 1979. "A Simple Model of the Kondratieff Cycle." In *Research in Economic History,* Vol. 4, P. Ulselding, ed., pp. 1–36. Greenwich, Conn.: JAI Press.

Rothschild-Whitt, Joyce. 1979. "The Collectivist Organization: An Alternative to Rational-Bureaucratic Models." *American Sociological Review* 44, no. 4: 509–27.

Scherer, F. M. 1980. *Industrial Market Structure and Economic Performance.* 2nd edition. Chicago: Rand McNally.

Schumpeter, Joseph A. 1961. *The Theory of Economic Development.* New York: Oxford University Press.

_____. 1950. *Capitalism, Socialism, and Democracy.* New York: Harper and Row.

_____. 1939. *Business Cycles.* New York: McGraw-Hill.

Schweikart, David. 1982. *Capitalism or Worker Control.* New York: Praeger.

Sheppard, Harold L., and Neal Q. Herrick. 1972. *Where Have All the Robots Gone: Worker Dissatisfaction in the '70s.* New York: Free Press.

Soma, John T. 1976. *The Computer Industry.* Lexington, Mass.: Lexington Books.

Stein, Barry A. 1976. "Rebuilding Bedford-Stuyvesant: Community Economic Development in the Ghetto." Cambridge, Mass.: Center for Community Economic Development.

_____. 1974. *Size, Efficiency, and Community Enterprise.* Cambridge, Mass.: Center for Community Economic Development.

Stephen, Frank H. 1984. *The Economic Analysis of Producers' Cooperatives.* New York: St. Martin's Press.

———. 1982. "The Economic Theory of the Labour-managed Firm." In *The Performance of Labour-Managed Firms,* Frank H. Stephen, ed., pp. 3–26. New York: St. Martin's Press.

Stewart, James B. 1984. "Building a Cooperative Economy: Lessons from the Black Experience." *Review of Social Economy,* December, pp. 360–68.

Sussman, Carl. 1980. "Founding the Community Development Finance Corporation." In *Developing the Public Economy: Models from Massachusetts,* Pat McGuigan and Bob Schaeffer, eds., pp. 81–92. Cambridge, Mass.: Policy Training Center.

Thomas, Hendrik. 1982. "The Performance of the Mondragon Cooperatives in Spain." In *Participatory and Self-Managed Firms,* Derek Jones and Jan Svejnar, eds., pp. 129–51. Lexington, Mass.: Lexington Books.

Thomas, Henk and Chris Logan, *Mondragon: An Economic Analysis,* London: Allen and Unwin, 1982.

U.S. Advisory Commission on Intergovernmental Relations. 1983. *1981 Tax Capacity of the Fifty States.* Washington, D.C.: U.S. Government Printing Office.

———. 1962. "Measures of State and Local Fiscal Capacity and Tax Effort." Washington, D.C.: U.S. Government Printing Office.

U.S. Bureau of the Census. 1960–1940. *Census of Population: Manufactures.* Washington, D.C.: U.S. Government Printing Office.

———. 1954–1983. *Statistical Abstract of the United States.* Washington, D.C.: U.S. Government Printing Office.

Van Duijn, J. J. 1983. *The Long Wave in Economic Life.* New York: George Allen and Unwin.

Vanek, Jaroslav. 1977. *The Labor-Managed Economy.* Ithaca, N.Y.: Cornell University Press.

Ward, Benjamin. 1958. "The Firm in Illyria: Market Syndicalism." *American Economic Review,* September, pp. 566–89.

Watkins, Alfred J. 1980. *The Practice of Urban Economics.* Beverly Hills, Calif.: Sage.

Webb, Beatrice. 1891. *The Cooperative Movement.* London: Swann Sonnenschein.

Webb, Sidney, and Beatrice Webb. 1921. *The Consumers' Cooperative Movement.* London: Longmans, Green and Co.

Wessel, David. 1984. "Calculated Change." *Wall Street Journal,* November 6, p. 1.

Williamson, Oliver E. 1975. *Markets and Hierarchies: Analysis and Antitrust Implications.* New York: The Free Press.

Wilson, Robert W., Peter K. Ashton, and Thomas P. Egan. 1980. *Innovation, Competition, and Government Policy in the Semiconductor Industry.* Lexington, Mass.: Lexington Books.

Work in America. 1973. Report of a Special Task Force to the Secretary of Health, Education and Welfare. Cambridge, Mass.: MIT Press.

Zevi, Alberto. 1982. "The Performance of Italian Producer Cooperatives." In *Participatory and Self-Managed Firms,* Derek Jones and Jan Svejnar, eds., pp. 239–51. Lexington, Mass.: Lexington Books.

INDEX